Python Programming Essentials *Build Real-World Applications from Scratch*

A Step-by-Step Guide to Mastering Python for Developers

MIGUEL FARMER

RAFAEL SANDERS

Table of Content

TABLE OF CONTENTS

INTRODUCTION

Python Programming Essentials

Welcome to **"Python Programming Essentials: Build Real-World Applications from Scratch"** — a comprehensive guide designed to take you on an immersive journey through Python programming, from foundational concepts to advanced techniques, empowering you to build real-world applications. Whether you're a beginner just stepping into the world of programming or an experienced developer looking to sharpen your skills, this book is crafted to suit all levels, guiding you through practical and insightful examples along the way.

Python has firmly established itself as one of the most versatile, beginner-friendly, and powerful programming languages. With its clear and readable syntax, vast ecosystem of libraries, and widespread use across industries, Python is the go-to language for a variety of applications, including web development, data analysis, machine learning, automation, and more. The demand for Python developers continues to rise, and mastering it opens up a world of opportunities in numerous domains.

This book is structured to provide both **theoretical understanding** and **hands-on experience** through real-world projects, ensuring that you not only grasp the fundamentals but also develop the confidence to apply your knowledge to solve practical problems.

What You Will Learn in This Book

Throughout this book, you will explore key topics and technologies that will enhance your programming and software development skills:

1. **Getting Started with Python**:
    o   Setting up the Python environment across different platforms.
    o   Understanding basic syntax and data types, including integers, strings, lists, and dictionaries.
    o   Writing and running simple Python programs.
2. **Control Flow and Functions**:

- o Mastering conditional statements and loops to control the flow of your code.
- o Writing reusable and efficient functions, passing arguments, and handling return values.
- o Implementing error handling and exceptions to ensure robust code.

3. **Object-Oriented Programming (OOP)**:
   - o Learning the core principles of OOP: classes, objects, inheritance, polymorphism, and encapsulation.
   - o Designing and building object-oriented applications that are maintainable and scalable.

4. **Working with Data**:
   - o Handling data structures like lists, tuples, sets, and dictionaries effectively.
   - o Exploring external data through APIs and integrating with databases like SQLite, MySQL, or MongoDB.
   - o Working with CSV, JSON, and XML files for data parsing and processing.

5. **Web Development with Flask**:

- Building web applications using the Flask framework.
- Implementing basic API endpoints and interacting with databases.
- Creating dynamic and interactive websites using HTML, CSS, and JavaScript.

6. **Testing and Debugging**:
   - Writing unit tests with frameworks like `unittest` and `pytest` to ensure code reliability.
   - Using Python's built-in debugger `pdb` and IDE tools to debug and resolve issues in your code.

7. **Automation and Scaling Applications**:
   - Automating repetitive tasks with Python scripts and scheduling jobs using libraries like `schedule` and `APScheduler`.
   - Scaling your applications with containerization tools like Docker for deployment on cloud platforms such as Heroku or AWS.

8. **Final Project**:
   - Putting everything together to build a **full-stack web application**, integrating a Flask

backend, a frontend UI, and a database, and deploying it for production use.

Why Python? Why This Book?

Python's **simplicity** and **flexibility** have made it a favorite among developers, data scientists, and engineers worldwide. The language's design philosophy emphasizes readability and ease of use, which makes it perfect for both beginners and seasoned professionals. This book leverages Python's strengths to provide you with a clear, concise, and engaging learning experience.

What sets this book apart is its **project-based learning approach**. You won't just be reading about concepts — you will actively work on building functional applications. From a **task manager app** to a **Flask-based web application**, you will explore how to apply Python's core features in practical scenarios, step by step. Each chapter focuses on clear explanations, real-world examples, and hands-on exercises that will leave you with a concrete understanding of Python programming.

Whether you want to build web applications, automate your workflow, analyze data, or dive into machine learning, **"Python Programming Essentials"** will provide the foundation for you to tackle any project.

Who This Book Is For

This book is designed for:

- **Beginners** with little or no experience in programming. The book takes a **gradual approach**, starting from the basics of Python and progressing to more advanced topics.
- **Intermediate Python programmers** who want to deepen their knowledge and learn best practices for writing clean, efficient code.
- **Developers** who want to expand their skill set and build real-world applications using Python.
- **Students** looking for a practical, project-based guide to learning Python programming and software development.

How to Use This Book

Each chapter in this book builds on the previous one, allowing you to gradually progress from basic Python concepts to more advanced application development. However, you can also choose to skip around based on your current knowledge and interests.

- **Follow the Examples**: Each concept comes with hands-on examples, which you should follow along with on your own machine. Running the code and experimenting with it will help solidify your understanding.
- **Work on the Projects**: At the end of each section, you will be tasked with building real-world projects. These projects will give you experience applying what you've learned to solve real problems.
- **Challenge Yourself**: We've included challenges and bonus tasks at the end of many chapters. These tasks will help you reinforce your learning and explore new concepts in more depth.

What's Inside

- **Detailed explanations** of Python's core concepts with easy-to-follow examples.
- **Hands-on projects** that will teach you how to build functional applications with Flask, automate tasks, and work with databases.
- **Real-world case studies** that demonstrate how Python can be used in various domains such as web development, data science, and automation.
- **Best practices** for writing clean, maintainable, and scalable Python code.
- **Practical tips** on debugging, testing, and deploying Python applications.

Conclusion

By the end of this book, you will have mastered the fundamental skills needed to develop real-world Python applications. Whether you are building a personal project, automating everyday tasks, or working on professional web development, **Python Programming Essentials** will equip you with the tools and knowledge to succeed. Let's get started on this exciting journey of Python programming and build something amazing!

CHAPTER 1

WELCOME TO PYTHON PROGRAMMING

Introduction to Python and Its Importance in the Programming World

Welcome to Python programming! Whether you're just starting your coding journey or looking to expand your skills, Python is an excellent choice. It is one of the most popular and versatile programming languages in the world, used by developers, data scientists, engineers, and even creatives.

Python was created by **Guido van Rossum** in the late 1980s and was first released in 1991. Its simple, readable syntax and dynamic typing system made it an instant hit. Unlike other programming languages that can be verbose or tricky to learn, Python has a clean and concise syntax, making it easy for beginners to grasp while still being powerful enough for experts to build sophisticated applications.

Today, Python is used in a variety of fields, ranging from simple scripting tasks to advanced machine learning projects. Its flexibility and powerful libraries have made it the go-to choice for many industries and tech companies.

Key Features and Why Python is Beginner-Friendly

1. **Simple** **Syntax**

   One of Python's standout features is its simple and readable syntax. For beginners, Python's code looks like plain English, which makes it easier to write and understand. The use of indentation rather than braces { } to define code blocks makes the structure intuitive and user-friendly.

   Example:

   ```python
   python

   if temperature > 30:
       print("It's a hot day!")
   else:
       print("It's a cool day!")
   ```

   As you can see, Python's syntax eliminates the need for many formalities that other programming languages might require, such as semicolons at the end of lines or curly braces around code blocks.

2. **Large   Community   and   Support**

Python has a large and active community of developers. This means that you have access to a wealth of learning resources, tutorials, and third-party libraries. If you ever encounter a challenge, chances are that someone else has faced it and solved it. You can easily find solutions on forums like **Stack Overflow** or through official Python documentation.

3. **Cross-Platform   Compatibility**

Python is cross-platform, which means it can run on any operating system—Windows, macOS, Linux, or even mobile devices. The code you write will work on any machine with a Python interpreter installed, making it highly portable for developers.

4. **Extensive   Libraries   and   Frameworks**

Python's ecosystem includes a vast collection of libraries and frameworks that you can use to build projects quickly and efficiently. Libraries like **NumPy**, **pandas**, and **Matplotlib** make Python a powerful tool for data analysis, while frameworks like **Flask** and **Django** allow you to build web applications effortlessly.

5. **High-Level   Language**

Python abstracts away many of the complex details of the computer's internal workings. You don't need to worry about memory management or low-level operations, which allows you to focus on solving problems rather than handling technical details.

Python Use Cases: Web Development, Data Science, AI, Automation, and More

Python's versatility is one of the reasons it's such a popular language. Below are some of the primary use cases for Python, demonstrating its broad application in different fields:

1. **Web** **Development**

   Python is an excellent choice for building websites and web applications. Frameworks like **Django** and **Flask** provide developers with powerful tools to create dynamic web pages, user authentication systems, and APIs, all with relatively simple code. Python's simplicity makes it especially appealing for building scalable and maintainable web applications.

   Example: A popular website like **Instagram** was originally built using Python and the Django framework. Django helped manage complex databases and provided a quick way to build features like messaging, notifications, and user feeds.

2. **Data Science and Analytics**

Python is the go-to language for **data science** and **data analysis**. With libraries such as **pandas** for data manipulation, **NumPy** for numerical computing, and **Matplotlib** for data visualization, Python makes it easy to work with large datasets. Whether it's cleaning data, performing statistical analysis, or creating beautiful charts, Python is designed to handle it all.

Example: Data scientists use Python to analyze data from various sources, build predictive models, and create visualizations to present insights. For instance, a data analyst at a company might use Python to analyze customer purchasing behavior to improve marketing strategies.

3. **Artificial Intelligence and Machine Learning**

Python has become one of the most prominent languages in the field of **AI and machine learning**. Libraries like **TensorFlow, Keras,** and **scikit-learn** provide pre-built tools and algorithms to make machine learning accessible to developers. Python's clean syntax allows researchers and developers to experiment with cutting-edge AI models easily.

Example: Companies like **Google, Netflix,** and **Amazon** use Python to implement machine learning algorithms.

For example, Python helps Netflix recommend shows to viewers based on their viewing history using machine learning models.

4. **Automation**   **and**   **Scripting**

Python is often used to automate repetitive tasks or create scripts to handle system operations. For example, you can write Python scripts to automate data entry tasks, scrape data from websites, or even manage server infrastructure.

Example: An IT administrator might write a Python script to automatically back up files, clean up system logs, or deploy updates across multiple servers.

5. **Game**   **Development**

While not as commonly used for game development as languages like C++ or Unity, Python can still be used to create simple 2D games or game prototypes. Libraries such as **Pygame** are great for hobbyists and indie developers looking to build games.

Example: A small game like **Flappy Bird** can be easily developed using Python and the Pygame library, where you focus more on the gameplay and mechanics rather than dealing with complex low-level programming.

6. **Scientific**   **Computing**

Python is widely used in scientific fields for numerical

simulations, solving mathematical problems, and visualizing scientific data. Libraries like **SciPy** and **SymPy** make Python a powerful tool for scientific research and engineering applications.

Example: Scientists might use Python to simulate the movement of molecules in a drug design process or to perform statistical analysis on biological data.

Conclusion

Python is a powerful, beginner-friendly, and versatile language that is applicable across many domains. Whether you're building a website, analyzing data, creating AI models, automating tasks, or exploring scientific simulations, Python provides the tools and simplicity necessary to tackle real-world problems. In the next chapters, we'll dive deeper into how to start writing Python code, from setting up your environment to working with Python's built-in features.

Are you ready to take your first steps into Python programming? Let's get started!

This chapter introduces Python, covering its significance and use cases, and highlights how Python's simplicity makes it a great choice for both beginners and experts. By the end of this chapter, readers should have a clear understanding of why Python is important and how it can be used in various fields.

CHAPTER 2

SETTING UP YOUR PYTHON ENVIRONMENT

Installation of Python on Different Operating Systems

Before you can start writing Python code, you need to install Python and set up the environment on your machine. The installation process differs slightly depending on the operating system you're using. In this section, we'll guide you through the process for **Windows, macOS**, and **Linux**.

1. Installing Python on Windows

Step 1: Download Python

- Go to the official Python website: https://www.python.org/downloads/.
- Click the **Download Python** button (it should detect the appropriate version for your system).

Step 2: Run the Installer

- After downloading, run the installer. During the installation process, make sure to check the box that says **"Add Python to PATH"**. This ensures that Python is accessible from the command line without having to specify the installation path.
- Click on **Install Now**. The installer will install Python and set it up correctly on your system.

Step 3: Verify the Installation

- Open the **Command Prompt** (you can search for cmd in the start menu).
- Type `python --version` and press Enter. If everything was set up correctly, you should see something like this:

```
nginx
```

```
Python 3.x.x
```

Step 4: Installing pip

- The Python installer typically includes **pip**, the package installer for Python. To verify pip is installed, run the following command:

```
css
```

```
pip --version
```

2. Installing Python on macOS

Step 1: Download Python

- Visit the official Python website: https://www.python.org/downloads/.
- Download the latest Python version for macOS.

Step 2: Run the Installer

- Open the downloaded .pkg file and follow the on-screen instructions to install Python on your Mac.

Step 3: Verify the Installation

- Open the **Terminal** (you can search for it in Spotlight).
- Type python3 --version and press Enter. You should see something like:

```
nginx
```

```
Python 3.x.x
```

Step 4: Installing pip

- macOS typically includes pip by default. To confirm it is installed, type:

```
css
```

25

```
pip3 --version
```

---

3. Installing Python on Linux

On Linux, the installation process can vary depending on the distribution you're using. Here's how to install Python on **Ubuntu** (most common Linux distribution).

Step 1: Install Python Using APT

- Open a **Terminal**.
- Update the package list:

```
sql
```

```
sudo apt update
```

- Install Python 3 by running the following command:

```
nginx
```

```
sudo apt install python3
```

Step 2: Verify the Installation

- Check the installed version of Python by running:

```
css
```

26

```
python3 --version
```

Step 3: Installing pip

- To install `pip` for Python 3, run:

```
nginx
```

```
sudo apt install python3-pip
```

- Verify the installation of `pip`:

```
css
```

```
pip3 --version
```

Introduction to Integrated Development Environments (IDEs)

Now that you've installed Python, you'll need an **Integrated Development Environment (IDE)** to write, edit, and run your Python code efficiently. There are several great IDEs available, and we'll introduce three of the most popular: **VS Code**, **PyCharm**, and **Jupyter Notebook**.

---

1. Visual Studio Code (VS Code)

VS Code is a lightweight and powerful code editor developed by Microsoft. It's highly customizable and supports Python through extensions, making it a great choice for both beginners and advanced developers.

Step 1: Install VS Code

- Visit the VS Code download page.
- Choose the version for your operating system and install it.

Step 2: Install the Python Extension

- Open VS Code, go to the Extensions tab (on the left side), and search for "Python."
- Install the official Python extension by Microsoft.

Step 3: Configure VS Code for Python

- Open a folder or workspace in VS Code where you want to save your Python projects.
- When you first open a Python file (.py), VS Code will prompt you to install additional Python-related tools, like **Pylint** for linting and **Jupyter** for running notebooks. Install these tools as recommended.

Step 4: Running Your Python Code

- To run a Python file, simply open the file in VS Code and click the **Run** button in the top right corner, or open the terminal within VS Code and type:

```php-template

python <your-file-name.py>
```

2. PyCharm

PyCharm is a full-featured IDE developed by JetBrains specifically for Python development. It is available in two versions: the free **Community** version and the paid **Professional** version.

Step 1: Install PyCharm

- Download the latest version of PyCharm from the official site.
- Install the version suitable for your operating system.

Step 2: Configure PyCharm

- Once installed, launch PyCharm and set up your first Python project by creating a new **Python project** in the IDE.
- PyCharm automatically detects your Python installation and configures the environment.

29

Step 3: Running Your Python Code

- Simply right-click the Python file in the **Project** pane and select **Run** to execute your Python code. You can also use the **Run** button at the top of the interface.

---

3. Jupyter Notebook

Jupyter Notebook is a web-based application for creating and sharing documents that contain live code, equations, visualizations, and explanatory text. It's ideal for data analysis, scientific research, and learning Python interactively.

Step 1: Install Jupyter Notebook

- First, you need to install **Jupyter** using `pip`:

```
nginx
```

```
pip install notebook
```

Step 2: Running Jupyter Notebook

- In your terminal or command prompt, type:

```
nginx
```

```
jupyter notebook
```

- This will open a browser window where you can create, edit, and run Python notebooks.

Step 3: Writing Code in Jupyter Notebook

- Once the notebook interface opens in your browser, click **New > Python 3** to create a new notebook.
- You can write and execute Python code within cells. To run a cell, press **Shift + Enter**.

Running Your First Python Script

Now that you've set up your Python environment and chosen an IDE, let's write and run your first Python script.

Step 1: Writing Your First Python Program

Let's write a simple program that prints **Hello, World!**.

1. Open your IDE of choice (VS Code, PyCharm, or Jupyter Notebook).
2. Create a new Python file and name it `hello_world.py`.
3. Type the following code inside the file:

```python

print("Hello, World!")
```

Step 2: Running the Program

- In **VS Code** or **PyCharm**, open the terminal or use the **Run** button.
- In **Jupyter Notebook**, run the cell containing the code by pressing **Shift + Enter**.

Once you run the code, you should see the output:

```
Hello, World!
```

Congratulations! You've just written and executed your first Python program!

Conclusion

In this chapter, we've walked you through the steps of setting up Python on your system, introduced you to three popular IDEs (VS Code, PyCharm, and Jupyter Notebook), and helped you run your first Python script. Now that your environment is set up and you're familiar with your tools, you can move forward to learn more about Python and start building your own projects. In the next chapter, we'll dive deeper into Python's basic syntax and data types. Happy coding!

CHAPTER 3

PYTHON BASICS: SYNTAX AND STRUCTURE

Understanding Python Syntax and Structure

Python is known for its clean, easy-to-read syntax. This simplicity is one of the reasons why Python is often recommended for beginners. Let's start by understanding how Python code is structured.

1. Indentation in Python

In Python, indentation is not just for readability; it defines the structure of your code. Unlike many programming languages that use braces { } to indicate code blocks, Python uses **indentation** (whitespace) to group statements into blocks.

- **Indentation Levels**: The standard indentation level is four spaces, but you can also use tabs as long as they are consistent throughout your code.

Example:

```
python

if 5 > 2:
    print("Five is greater than two!")
```

In the example above, the `print` statement is indented to indicate that it is part of the `if` block. Without the indentation, Python would raise an error.

---

2. Python Comments

Comments are lines of text that are ignored by Python. They're useful for documenting your code, explaining what it does, and keeping track of changes.

- **Single-line Comments**: Use # to write a comment on a single line.
- **Multi-line Comments**: Use triple quotes (""" or ''') for multi-line comments.

Example:

```
python

# This is a single-line comment
print("Hello, World!")    # This prints to the
console
```

34

```
"""
This is a multi-line comment.
It can span across several lines.
"""
```

Comments are crucial for making your code more understandable, especially as it grows larger.

---

3. Case Sensitivity

Python is **case-sensitive**, which means that `Variable` and `variable` are considered different identifiers.

Example:

```python
python

variable = 10
Variable = 20
print(variable)   # Output: 10
print(Variable)   # Output: 20
```

This case sensitivity is important to keep in mind as you define variables and function names.

Variables and Basic Data Types

In Python, a **variable** is a name that is used to reference a value stored in memory. Python is dynamically typed, which means you don't have to explicitly declare the type of a variable. The type is inferred based on the value assigned to it.

---

1. Variables

You can assign a value to a variable by using the = operator.

Example:

```python
x = 5  # Assigning the value 5 to variable x
name = "Alice"  # Assigning the string "Alice" to variable name
```

In Python, you can assign multiple variables at once:

```python
x, y, z = 1, 2, 3  # Assigning values to multiple variables
```

---

2. Basic Data Types

36

Python has several built-in data types. Let's look at the most common ones:

---

a. **Integers**

An **integer** is a whole number without a decimal point.

Example:

```python
age = 25   # An integer
```

---

b. **Floats**

A **float** (short for floating-point number) is a number that has a decimal point.

Example:

```python
price = 19.99   # A float
temperature = 22.5   # A float
```

---

c. **Strings**

A **string** is a sequence of characters enclosed in either single quotes (') or double quotes (").

Example:

```python
```

```python
name = "John"   # A string
message = 'Hello, Python!'   # Another way to
define a string
```

Strings can also include escape characters, such as \n for a new line or \t for a tab.

Example:

```python
```

```python
greeting = "Hello, \nWorld!"
print(greeting)
```

This will print:

```
Hello,
World!
```

d. **Booleans**

A **boolean** is a data type that can have one of two values: `True` or
`False`.

Example:

```python

is_sunny = True   # A boolean
is_raining = False   # Another boolean
```

Booleans are commonly used for decision-making, such as in
conditional statements (`if` statements).

How to Write and Run Simple Python Programs

Now that we've covered the basics of Python syntax, structure, and
data types, let's write and run a simple Python program. We'll start
with a basic program that takes user input and performs some
simple calculations.

Example 1: Hello, World!

This is the classic first program you write in any programming
language. It simply prints **Hello, World!** to the console.

```
python
```

```
print("Hello, World!")
```

To run the program:

- **In VS Code** or **PyCharm**, open the terminal, navigate to the directory where the file is saved, and type:

```
nginx
```

```
python hello_world.py
```

- **In Jupyter Notebook**, simply run the cell with the `print` statement.

The output will be:

```
Hello, World!
```

Example 2: A Simple Calculator

Here's a program that prompts the user for two numbers, adds them together, and displays the result.

```
python
```

```
# Simple calculator program
```

40

```python
num1 = float(input("Enter the first number: "))
# Take first input
num2 = float(input("Enter the second number: "))
# Take second input

sum_result = num1 + num2   # Add the two numbers
print("The sum of", num1, "and", num2, "is",
sum_result)   # Print the result
```

Explanation:

- input() is used to take user input. By default, it returns the input as a **string**. To convert it to a number, we use float() for decimal numbers or int() for integers.
- print() is used to display the output.

Example 3: Using Variables and Basic Arithmetic

In this example, we will calculate the area of a rectangle using variables and basic arithmetic.

python

```python
# Calculate the area of a rectangle
length = 5  # length of the rectangle
width = 3   # width of the rectangle
```

```
area = length * width  # Area formula: length *
width
print("The area of the rectangle is", area)
```

Explanation:

- We define two variables (`length` and `width`), calculate the area by multiplying them, and then print the result.

The output will be:

csharp

```
The area of the rectangle is 15
```

Conclusion

In this chapter, we've covered the foundational elements of Python programming:

- **Python syntax and structure**, including indentation and comments.
- **Variables** and basic **data types** (integers, floats, strings, booleans), and how to use them effectively.
- How to write and run simple Python programs, including a "Hello, World!" program, a basic calculator, and a simple area calculator.

These concepts are the building blocks of Python programming, and mastering them will set you up for success as you dive deeper into more complex topics. In the next chapter, we'll explore **control flow**, which will allow you to write programs that can make decisions and repeat actions.

CHAPTER 4

WORKING WITH DATA TYPES AND VARIABLES

1. Detailed Exploration of Data Types

In Python, data types are used to specify what kind of value a variable can hold. Python has several built-in data types, and understanding them is crucial for writing efficient and readable code. In this section, we'll dive deeper into four important data types: **Lists**, **Tuples**, **Dictionaries**, and **Sets**.

1.1 Lists

A **list** is an ordered collection of items, which can be of different data types (integers, strings, etc.). Lists are **mutable**, meaning their contents can be changed after they are created.

- Lists are created using square brackets [].
- Items in a list are indexed, starting from 0.
- Lists can contain duplicate values.

Example:

44

```python
python

# Creating a list
fruits = ["apple", "banana", "cherry", "apple"]

# Accessing list elements by index
print(fruits[0])   # Output: apple

# Modifying a list
fruits[1] = "orange"
print(fruits)    # Output: ['apple', 'orange',
'cherry', 'apple']

# Adding an item to the list
fruits.append("grape")
print(fruits)    # Output: ['apple', 'orange',
'cherry', 'apple', 'grape']

# Removing an item from the list
fruits.remove("apple")
print(fruits)    # Output: ['orange', 'cherry',
'apple', 'grape']
```

Key operations with lists:

- append(): Adds an item at the end.
- remove(): Removes the first occurrence of a value.
- pop(): Removes an item by index and returns it.
- sort(): Sorts the list in ascending order.

45

1.2 Tuples

A **tuple** is similar to a list but **immutable**, meaning once created, you cannot change, add, or remove elements. Tuples are created using parentheses `()`.

- Tuples are ordered and indexed, like lists, but their contents cannot be modified.
- Tuples can contain duplicate values.

Example:

python

```
# Creating a tuple
colors = ("red", "green", "blue")

# Accessing tuple elements by index
print(colors[1])  # Output: green

# Attempting to modify a tuple (this will raise
an error)
# colors[1] = "yellow"  # Uncommenting this will
raise a TypeError
```

Key operations with tuples:

- `count()`: Returns the number of occurrences of a specified element.
- `index()`: Returns the index of the first occurrence of a specified element.

Tuples are often used when you want to store data that shouldn't be changed, such as coordinates or fixed collections of items.

1.3 Dictionaries

A **dictionary** is an unordered collection of key-value pairs. Keys in a dictionary must be unique and immutable (e.g., strings, numbers, or tuples), while the values can be of any data type.

- Dictionaries are created using curly braces `{}` and key-value pairs separated by a colon `:`.
- Items in a dictionary are accessed using keys, not indexes.

Example:

python

```
# Creating a dictionary
person = {"name": "Alice", "age": 30, "city":
"New York"}

# Accessing values by keys
```

```
print(person["name"])  # Output: Alice

# Adding a new key-value pair
person["job"] = "Engineer"
print(person)  # Output: {'name': 'Alice', 'age':
30, 'city': 'New York', 'job': 'Engineer'}

# Modifying a value
person["age"] = 31
print(person)  # Output: {'name': 'Alice', 'age':
31, 'city': 'New York', 'job': 'Engineer'}

# Removing a key-value pair
del person["city"]
print(person)  # Output: {'name': 'Alice', 'age':
31, 'job': 'Engineer'}
```

Key operations with dictionaries:

- `keys()`: Returns a list of all keys.
- `values()`: Returns a list of all values.
- `get()`: Retrieves the value for a specified key, and returns `None` if the key doesn't exist.
- `items()`: Returns all key-value pairs as a list of tuples.

Dictionaries are ideal for storing data that is associated with unique identifiers, such as user information or configuration settings.

1.4 Sets

A **set** is an unordered collection of unique elements. Sets are **mutable**, meaning you can add and remove elements, but they do not allow duplicates.

- Sets are created using curly braces { }.
- Items in a set are not indexed or ordered, and they cannot contain duplicate values.

Example:

python

```python
# Creating a set
colors_set = {"red", "green", "blue"}

# Adding an item to the set
colors_set.add("yellow")
print(colors_set)   # Output: {'blue', 'green', 'red', 'yellow'}

# Removing an item from the set
colors_set.remove("green")
print(colors_set)   # Output: {'blue', 'red', 'yellow'}
```

```
# Sets automatically ignore duplicates
colors_set.add("red")
print(colors_set)    # Output: {'blue', 'red',
'yellow'}
```

Key operations with sets:

- `add()`: Adds a new element to the set.
- `remove()`: Removes a specified element.
- `union()`: Combines two sets.
- `intersection()`: Returns the common elements between two sets.

Sets are often used when you want to eliminate duplicate values from a collection or perform mathematical set operations like union or intersection.

2. Variables: Naming Conventions, Mutability vs Immutability, Scope

2.1 Naming Conventions for Variables

Python variables should be named according to the following conventions:

- **Descriptive names**: Variables should have names that describe their purpose (e.g., `age`, `user_name`).

- **Lowercase with underscores**: Use lowercase letters and separate words with underscores for readability (e.g., `first_name`, `total_amount`).

- **Avoid reserved words**: Python has reserved keywords that cannot be used as variable names, such as `if`, `else`, `True`, `class`, etc.

- **Avoid starting with numbers**: Variable names cannot begin with a number, such as `2nd_name`.

Example:

```python
python

user_name = "John"
user_age = 25
total_amount = 100.50
```

2.2 Mutability vs Immutability

Understanding **mutability** (whether the object can be changed after creation) is crucial in Python.

- **Mutable** objects: **Lists**, **Dictionaries**, and **Sets** are mutable, meaning you can change their content after creation.

Example:

```python
my_list = [1, 2, 3]
my_list[0] = 100   # This is allowed
```

- **Immutable** objects: **Tuples**, **Strings**, and **Numbers** are immutable, meaning once you create them, their values cannot be changed.

Example:

```python
my_tuple = (1, 2, 3)
my_tuple[0] = 100   # This will raise a
TypeError
```

Immutability is useful in certain situations where you want to prevent accidental modification of values, such as when passing data to functions or working with constant values.

2.3 Variable Scope

The **scope** of a variable refers to where it can be accessed within your program. Python has **global scope** and **local scope**:

- **Global variables** are declared outside functions and are accessible throughout the entire program.
- **Local variables** are declared inside a function and can only be accessed within that function.

Example:

```python

# Global variable
x = 10

def my_function():
    # Local variable
    y = 20
    print(x, y)  # Local scope can access global
variable

my_function()
# print(y)  # This would raise a NameError because
y is local to my_function.
```

3. Practical Examples with Each Data Type

Let's combine all the concepts and see how we can work with these data types in a practical scenario.

Example 1: Store User Information in a Dictionary

python

```python
user_info = {
    "name": "Alice",
    "age": 30,
    "city": "New York",
    "interests":       ["coding",       "reading",
"traveling"]
}

# Adding a new key-value pair
user_info["job"] = "Engineer"

# Accessing and printing user info
print(user_info)
```

Example 2: Working with a List of Numbers

python

```python
numbers = [1, 2, 3, 4, 5]

# Appending a new number to the list
numbers.append(6)

# Loop through the list and print each number
for number in numbers:
    print(number)
```

Example 3: Handling Immutable Data Types

python

```python
# Tuple representing coordinates (x, y)
coordinates = (10, 20)

# Attempt to modify a tuple (this will raise an
error)
# coordinates[0] = 15  # Uncommenting this will
raise TypeError
```

Example 4: Performing Set Operations

python

```python
set1 = {1, 2, 3}
set2 = {3, 4, 5}

# Union of two sets
union_set = set1.union(set2)
print(union_set)  # Output: {1, 2, 3, 4, 5}

# Intersection of two sets
intersection_set = set1.intersection(set2)
print(intersection_set)  # Output: {3}
```

Conclusion

In this chapter, we've explored the core data types in Python: **lists**, **tuples**, **dictionaries**, and **sets**. We discussed their characteristics, how to use them, and the differences between mutable and immutable data types. We also covered naming conventions for variables and how variable scope works in Python.

Understanding how to work with these data types is essential for building more complex applications. In the next chapter, we will dive into **control flow**, which will allow you to write code that makes decisions and repeats actions.

CHAPTER 5

CONDITIONAL STATEMENTS AND LOOPS

In this chapter, we will explore how to control the flow of your Python programs using **conditional statements** and **loops**. These fundamental concepts allow you to write programs that can make decisions and repeat tasks, which are essential for creating interactive and dynamic applications.

1. if, else, elif Statements: Making Decisions in Python

Conditional statements enable your program to make decisions based on certain conditions. In Python, these decisions are made using the `if`, `elif`, and `else` statements. Let's break them down:

1.1 if Statement

The `if` statement is used to check whether a specific condition is **True**. If the condition evaluates to **True**, the block of code inside the `if` statement is executed.

Syntax:

```python

if condition:
    # code to execute if the condition is True
```

Example:

```python

age = 18
if age >= 18:
    print("You are eligible to vote!")
```

In this example, the condition `age >= 18` is **True**, so the message "You are eligible to vote!" is printed.

1.2 else Statement

The `else` statement is used when the `if` condition evaluates to **False**. It provides an alternative block of code that will be executed if the `if` condition fails.

Syntax:

```python
```

```
if condition:
    # code to execute if the condition is True
else:
    # code to execute if the condition is False
```

Example:

```
python
```

```
age = 16
if age >= 18:
    print("You are eligible to vote!")
else:
    print("You are not eligible to vote yet.")
```

Here, the condition `age >= 18` is **False**, so the message "You are not eligible to vote yet." is printed.

1.3 elif Statement

The `elif` (short for "else if") statement allows you to check multiple conditions sequentially. If the first `if` condition is **False**, Python moves to the `elif` condition (if it exists) and checks it. If that's also **False**, it moves on to the next `elif` or finally the `else`.

Syntax:

```
python
```

```
if condition1:
    # code to execute if condition1 is True
elif condition2:
    # code to execute if condition2 is True
else:
    # code to execute if all conditions are False
```

Example:

```
python

age = 20
if age < 18:
    print("You are too young to vote.")
elif age >= 18 and age < 21:
    print("You are eligible to vote, but not
drink alcohol.")
else:
    print("You are eligible to vote and drink
alcohol.")
```

In this case, since age is 20, the second condition elif age >= 18 and age < 21 is **True**, so the message "You are eligible to vote, but not drink alcohol." is printed.

2. for and while Loops: Iterating Over Data Structures

Loops allow you to run a block of code multiple times, which is especially useful when working with data structures like lists, tuples, dictionaries, and sets.

2.1 for Loop

A `for` loop is used to iterate over a sequence (like a list, string, or range) and execute a block of code for each item in the sequence.

Syntax:

python

```python
for item in sequence:
    # code to execute for each item
```

Example:

python

```python
fruits = ["apple", "banana", "cherry"]
for fruit in fruits:
    print(fruit)
```

This will print each item in the list one by one:

```
nginx
```

```
apple
banana
cherry
```

Example 2: Using a `for` loop with a `range`

You can use the `range()` function to generate a sequence of numbers, which is useful when you want to loop a specific number of times.

```
python
```

```python
for i in range(5):
    print(i)
```

This will print:

```
0
1
2
3
4
```

2.2 while Loop

A `while` loop runs as long as a given condition is **True**. It's useful when you don't know in advance how many iterations you need to perform.

Syntax:

```python
while condition:
    # code to execute as long as condition is True
```

Example:

```python
count = 0
while count < 5:
    print(count)
    count += 1  # Increment count by 1
```

This will print:

```
0
1
2
3
4
```

Warning: Be careful with `while` loops. If the condition never becomes **False**, the loop will run forever, which results in an infinite loop.

---

3. Real-World Examples: Creating a Basic Decision-Making Application

Let's put what we've learned into practice by creating a simple decision-making application that uses both conditional statements and loops. Our goal is to write a program that helps a user decide what type of activity to do based on the weather, and loops until the user provides a valid input.

Example 1: A Weather Activity Recommender

python

```
while True:
    weather = input("What is the weather like
today? (sunny, rainy, snowy): ").lower()

    if weather == "sunny":
        print("Great day for a walk in the
park!")
        break
    elif weather == "rainy":
```

64

```
        print("Perfect day for reading a book
inside.")
        break
    elif weather == "snowy":
        print("How about a fun snowball fight?")
        break
    else:
        print("Sorry, I don't recognize that
weather. Please enter sunny, rainy, or snowy.")
```

Explanation:

- We ask the user for input on the weather using the input() function.
- Based on the weather input, the program makes a suggestion using if, elif, and else.
- The loop will keep running until a valid weather condition is provided.

Here's how the program works:

- If the user types "sunny", the message "Great day for a walk in the park!" is printed, and the loop breaks.
- If the user types "rainy", the message "Perfect day for reading a book inside." is printed, and the loop breaks.
- If the user types "snowy", the message "How about a fun snowball fight?" is printed, and the loop breaks.

- If the user types something invalid, the program keeps asking for valid input.

Example 2: Counting Down Timer with a `while` Loop

```python

import time

countdown = 5
while countdown > 0:
    print(countdown)
    time.sleep(1)   # Pauses for 1 second
    countdown -= 1

print("Time's up!")
```

Explanation:

- We use a `while` loop to create a countdown timer that prints numbers from 5 to 1.
- The `time.sleep(1)` function pauses the program for 1 second between each number.
- Once the countdown reaches 0, it prints "Time's up!" and the loop ends.

Conclusion

In this chapter, we covered the following important concepts:

- **Conditional statements** (`if`, `elif`, `else`) to make decisions based on conditions.
- **Loops** (`for` and `while`) to iterate over data and repeat tasks multiple times.
- We explored real-world examples, such as creating a weather-based activity recommender and a countdown timer.

Mastering conditional statements and loops is essential for building more complex and interactive programs. In the next chapter, we will explore **functions**, which allow you to organize your code into reusable blocks, making your programs more modular and easier to maintain.

CHAPTER 6

FUNCTIONS: WRITING REUSABLE CODE

In this chapter, we will explore **functions**, a powerful feature in Python that allows you to write reusable and modular code. Functions are essential for organizing code, improving readability, and reducing redundancy. By the end of this chapter, you will be able to define your own functions, use parameters and return values, and handle different types of arguments.

1. Defining Functions, Parameters, and Return Values

A **function** is a block of code that performs a specific task. Once defined, a function can be called multiple times, making it easier to reuse code.

1.1 Defining a Simple Function

In Python, a function is defined using the `def` keyword, followed by the function name and a pair of parentheses `()`. If the function takes parameters, they are defined inside the parentheses.

Syntax:

```python
python
```

```python
def function_name(parameters):
    # Code block
    return value
```

- **def**: This keyword is used to define a function.
- **function_name**: The name you give your function.
- **parameters**: Values you pass into the function. Parameters are optional; if the function doesn't need any input, you leave the parentheses empty.
- **return**: The `return` statement is used to send a result back from the function to the caller. If there's no `return`, the function will return `None` by default.

Example:

```python
python
```

```python
# Defining a simple function
def greet(name):
    return f"Hello, {name}!"
```

```
# Calling the function
print(greet("Alice"))
```

Output:

```
Hello, Alice!
```

In this example:

- The function `greet()` takes one parameter, `name`.
- The function returns a greeting string that includes the value passed in as the `name` argument.

1.2 Function Parameters and Arguments

- **Parameters**: These are the placeholders used in the function definition to accept input values.
- **Arguments**: These are the actual values you pass to the function when calling it.

Example:

```python
def add_numbers(a, b):
    return a + b
```

```
result = add_numbers(5, 3)
print(result)   # Output: 8
```

In this case:

- a and b are **parameters** of the function add_numbers.
- 5 and 3 are the **arguments** passed when calling the function.

---

2. Default Arguments, Keyword Arguments, and Variable-Length Arguments

Python provides flexibility in how you can pass arguments to functions, including **default arguments**, **keyword arguments**, and **variable-length arguments**.

2.1 Default Arguments

You can assign default values to function parameters. If the caller does not provide an argument for a parameter, the default value is used.

Example:

```python
```

```
def greet(name="Guest"):
    return f"Hello, {name}!"


print(greet())          # Output: Hello, Guest!
print(greet("Alice"))   # Output: Hello, Alice!
```

Here:

- The parameter name has a default value of "Guest".
- If no argument is provided when calling greet(), "Guest" is used.
- If a value is passed, it overrides the default value.

2.2 Keyword Arguments

In Python, you can pass arguments to functions using **keyword arguments**, where you specify the name of the parameter along with its value. This allows you to pass the arguments in any order, as long as you specify the parameter names.

Example:

python

```
def describe_pet(animal_type, pet_name):
    print(f"I    have    a    {animal_type}    named
{pet_name}.")
```

```
describe_pet(pet_name="Buddy",
animal_type="dog")
```

Here:

- The order of the arguments doesn't matter because we are using **keyword arguments**.
- The output will be: `I have a dog named Buddy.`

2.3 Variable-Length Arguments

Sometimes you don't know in advance how many arguments will be passed to a function. Python allows you to handle such situations using **variable-length arguments** with `*args` and `**kwargs`.

- **`*args`**: Collects additional positional arguments as a tuple.
- **`**kwargs`**: Collects additional keyword arguments as a dictionary.

Example of `*args`:

```python
def add_numbers(*args):
```

73

```
    total = 0
    for num in args:
        total += num
    return total
```

```
print(add_numbers(1, 2, 3))   # Output: 6
print(add_numbers(10, 20, 30, 40))   # Output: 100
```

In this example:

- `*args` allows the function `add_numbers` to accept any number of arguments.
- It then sums up all the arguments and returns the total.

Example of **kwargs:

python

```
def describe_person(**kwargs):
    for key, value in kwargs.items():
        print(f"{key}: {value}")
```

```
describe_person(name="John",            age=30,
occupation="Engineer")
```

Here:

- `**kwargs` collects keyword arguments into a dictionary.
- The output will be:

```makefile
name: John
age: 30
occupation: Engineer
```

---

3. Real-World Example: Writing a Function to Calculate Shipping Costs Based on Weight

Let's apply what we've learned by writing a function that calculates shipping costs based on the weight of the package. The shipping cost will be determined by different weight brackets: light, medium, and heavy.

Shipping Cost Calculation:

- Light (0-5kg): $10
- Medium (6-15kg): $20
- Heavy (16-30kg): $30
- Over 30kg: $50

We will use a function with **conditional statements** and **default arguments** to handle this.

Example:

```python
```

```python
def             calculate_shipping_cost(weight,
shipping_method="standard"):
    """
    Calculate shipping cost based on weight and
shipping method.
    :param weight: Weight of the package in
kilograms
    :param shipping_method: Method of shipping,
default is "standard"
    :return: The calculated shipping cost
    """
    if weight <= 5:
        cost = 10
    elif weight <= 15:
        cost = 20
    elif weight <= 30:
        cost = 30
    else:
        cost = 50


    # Adding an additional charge for express
shipping
    if shipping_method == "express":
        cost += 15  # Express shipping costs an
additional $15


    return cost


# Testing the function
```

```
weight = 8   # Example weight
method = "express"  # Example shipping method

cost = calculate_shipping_cost(weight, method)
print(f"The  shipping  cost  for  a  {weight}kg
package with {method} shipping is: ${cost}")
```

Explanation:

- The function `calculate_shipping_cost` takes two parameters: `weight` and `shipping_method`. `shipping_method` has a default value of `"standard"`.
- Based on the weight of the package, the function calculates the cost using a series of `if-elif` conditions.
- If the user chooses `"express"` shipping, an additional $15 is added to the total cost.

Example Output:

```pgsql
The shipping cost for a 8kg package with express
shipping is: $35
```

Conclusion

In this chapter, we learned how to write and use functions to make our code reusable and modular:

- **Defining functions** with parameters and return values.
- Understanding the use of **default arguments**, **keyword arguments**, and **variable-length arguments** (`*args` and `**kwargs`).
- We also applied these concepts by creating a real-world example of a function to calculate shipping costs based on the weight of a package.

Functions are a key part of writing clean, efficient, and reusable code. In the next chapter, we will explore **more advanced topics** such as working with file input/output and handling external data sources.

CHAPTER 7

HANDLING ERRORS AND EXCEPTIONS

Error handling is an essential part of writing robust Python programs. In this chapter, we will explore how to handle runtime errors gracefully using `try-except` blocks, create custom exceptions, and raise errors when necessary. We'll also walk through a real-world example of implementing error handling in a banking application.

1. Try-Except Blocks: Handling Runtime Errors Gracefully

In Python, **runtime errors** are errors that occur while the program is running, and they can cause your program to crash if not handled properly. Python provides a mechanism called **exception handling** to catch and handle these errors without crashing the program.

The most common way to handle exceptions in Python is by using `try-except` blocks.

1.1 Syntax of Try-Except Block

python

```
try:
    # Code that may raise an error
    risky_code()
except ExceptionType as e:
    # Code that runs if an error occurs
    print(f"An error occurred: {e}")
```

- **try**: The block of code you want to execute. If any error occurs in this block, Python will move to the except block.

- **except**: This block of code will execute if an error occurs in the try block. You can specify the type of exception you want to handle (e.g., ZeroDivisionError, ValueError).

- **ExceptionType**: Specifies the type of exception you want to handle (this is optional). If you want to catch all exceptions, use Exception.

- **as e**: This allows you to store the error message in a variable e, which you can then use for logging or displaying a user-friendly error message.

1.2 Example: Basic Try-Except Block

Let's see a simple example where we handle a division by zero error using a `try-except` block.

python

```
try:
    result = 10 / 0   # This will raise a
ZeroDivisionError
except ZeroDivisionError as e:
    print(f"Error: {e}")
```

Output:

vbnet

```
Error: division by zero
```

In this example:

- The code inside the `try` block attempts to divide 10 by 0, which raises a `ZeroDivisionError`.
- The `except` block catches the error and prints a message.

1.3 Handling Multiple Exceptions

You can also handle multiple types of exceptions by adding multiple `except` blocks.

```python
```

```python
try:
    num = int(input("Enter a number: "))   # May
raise ValueError if input is not a number
    result  =   10  /  num      #   May   raise
ZeroDivisionError
except ValueError as ve:
    print(f"Invalid input: {ve}")
except ZeroDivisionError as zde:
    print(f"Error: {zde}")
```

In this case, the program handles two possible errors:

1. **ValueError** if the user enters a non-integer value.
2. **ZeroDivisionError** if the user enters 0.

1.4 Finally Block

The `finally` block allows you to execute code that must run no matter what, whether or not an exception occurred. It's commonly used for cleanup activities, like closing files or releasing resources.

```python
```

```python
try:
```

```
num = int(input("Enter a number: "))
result = 10 / num
except ZeroDivisionError:
    print("Error: Division by zero!")
finally:
    print("This code runs no matter what.")
```

Output (if 0 is entered):

```
vbnet
```

```
Error: Division by zero!
This code runs no matter what.
```

---

2. Custom Exceptions and Raising Errors

Sometimes, built-in exceptions aren't enough to handle all error situations. In such cases, you can define your own **custom exceptions**. Custom exceptions allow you to raise and handle errors specific to your application.

2.1 Creating Custom Exceptions

To create a custom exception, you need to define a new class that inherits from Python's built-in `Exception` class. You can then use this class in your code to raise errors.

Syntax:

```python
python
```

```python
class CustomError(Exception):
    pass
```

Example: A custom exception for invalid withdrawal amounts in a banking application.

```python
python
```

```python
class InvalidAmountError(Exception):
    """Raised when the withdrawal amount is
negative or zero."""
    pass

def withdraw(amount):
    if amount <= 0:
        raise InvalidAmountError("Amount must be
greater than zero.")
    print(f"Withdrew {amount} dollars.")

try:
    withdraw(-100)
except InvalidAmountError as e:
    print(f"Error: {e}")
```

Output:

84

```
javascript
```

```
Error: Amount must be greater than zero.
```

In this example:

- We defined a custom exception `InvalidAmountError` that is raised when a withdrawal amount is less than or equal to zero.
- The `withdraw()` function raises this custom exception if the condition is met.

2.2 Raising Exceptions

In Python, you can raise exceptions using the `raise` keyword. This is useful when you want to trigger an error condition in your code.

```python
python
```

```python
def check_age(age):
    if age < 18:
        raise ValueError("You must be 18 or older
to access this content.")
    else:
        print("Access granted.")
```

85

```
try:
    check_age(16)
except ValueError as e:
    print(f"Error: {e}")
```

Output:

```
javascript
```

```
Error: You must be 18 or older to access this
content.
```

In this example:

- The `check_age()` function raises a `ValueError` if the user is under 18, and the exception is caught in the `except` block.

---

3. Real-World Example: Implementing Error Handling in a Banking Application

Let's now look at a real-world example of using error handling in a simple banking application. We will create a function to handle user withdrawals and ensure that no one can withdraw an amount greater than their balance.

Banking Application Example:

```python
python


class InsufficientFundsError(Exception):
    """Raised when an account has insufficient
funds for a withdrawal."""
    pass


class NegativeAmountError(Exception):
    """Raised when the withdrawal amount is
negative."""
    pass


class BankAccount:
    def __init__(self, balance):
        self.balance = balance

    def withdraw(self, amount):
        if amount <= 0:
            raise
NegativeAmountError("Withdrawal amount must be
positive.")
        if amount > self.balance:
            raise
InsufficientFundsError("Insufficient funds for
this withdrawal.")
        self.balance -= amount
        print(f"Successfully withdrew {amount}.
Remaining balance: {self.balance}")
```

87

```python
# Example usage
account = BankAccount(1000)

try:
    account.withdraw(1200)
except InsufficientFundsError as e:
    print(f"Error: {e}")

try:
    account.withdraw(-50)
except NegativeAmountError as e:
    print(f"Error: {e}")
```

Explanation:

- We created two custom exceptions: InsufficientFundsError and NegativeAmountError.
- The BankAccount class has a method withdraw(), which raises one of these exceptions depending on the situation.
- The first try block attempts to withdraw more money than the account balance, triggering the InsufficientFundsError.
- The second try block attempts to withdraw a negative amount, triggering the NegativeAmountError.

Output:

```
javascript
```

```
Error: Insufficient funds for this withdrawal.
Error: Withdrawal amount must be positive.
```

---

4. Conclusion

In this chapter, we covered the key aspects of error handling in Python:

- **Try-except blocks**: We learned how to handle runtime errors gracefully.
- **Custom exceptions**: We saw how to define and raise our own exceptions to handle specific error conditions.
- **Real-world example**: We implemented error handling in a banking application, demonstrating how to handle errors like insufficient funds and invalid withdrawal amounts.

By mastering error handling, you can write more reliable and user-friendly programs that can recover from unexpected situations without crashing. In the next chapter, we will explore **working with files** and how to handle input/output operations.

CHAPTER 8

UNDERSTANDING LIST COMPREHENSIONS

In this chapter, we will introduce **list comprehensions**, a powerful feature in Python that allows for more concise and efficient ways to create and manipulate lists. We'll also see how list comprehensions can enhance the readability of your code and boost performance. Lastly, we'll walk through a real-world example of processing data from a CSV file using list comprehensions.

1. Introduction to List Comprehensions for Efficient Looping

A **list comprehension** is a compact way to process and create lists in Python. It's an alternative to using traditional `for` loops and is designed to make code more readable and concise.

The general syntax of a list comprehension is as follows:

```python

[expression for item in iterable if condition]
```

- **expression**: The value or operation that you want to include in the new list.
- **item**: The variable representing each element in the iterable.
- **iterable**: The collection you are looping over (e.g., list, tuple, string, range).
- **condition** (optional): A condition that filters elements from the iterable based on a specified criterion.

1.1 Basic List Comprehension

Let's start with a simple example: creating a new list where each element is the square of the numbers in an existing list.

Example:

python

```
numbers = [1, 2, 3, 4, 5]
squares = [n**2 for n in numbers]
print(squares)   # Output: [1, 4, 9, 16, 25]
```

Here:

- n**2 is the expression that squares each number.
- for n in numbers is the loop that iterates through each number in the numbers list.

91

- The result is a new list with the squares of the numbers.

1.2 List Comprehension with a Condition

You can also add an **optional condition** to filter the items in the iterable. The condition is placed after the `for` loop.

Example: Creating a list of squares for only the even numbers in the `numbers` list.

```python

numbers = [1, 2, 3, 4, 5]
even_squares = [n**2 for n in numbers if n % 2 == 0]
print(even_squares)   # Output: [4, 16]
```

Here:

- The condition `if n % 2 == 0` ensures that only even numbers are included in the new list.
- The result is a list of squares of only the even numbers: `[4, 16]`.

2. How List Comprehensions Enhance Readability and Performance

List comprehensions make your code more **concise** and **readable** by eliminating the need for verbose `for` loops. In many cases, they also improve performance since they are optimized for creating lists efficiently.

2.1 Enhancing Readability

List comprehensions allow you to express complex operations in a single line, which can make the code easier to follow for someone familiar with Python.

For example, here's a traditional `for` loop that creates a list of even numbers:

python

```
even_numbers = []
for num in range(1, 11):
    if num % 2 == 0:
        even_numbers.append(num)
print(even_numbers)  # Output: [2, 4, 6, 8, 10]
```

Now, here's the same code using a list comprehension:

93

```python
```

```python
even_numbers = [num for num in range(1, 11) if
num % 2 == 0]
print(even_numbers)  # Output: [2, 4, 6, 8, 10]
```

As you can see, the list comprehension is much shorter and easier to understand at a glance. It's a more **elegant** and **Pythonic** way of writing the same logic.

2.2 Improving Performance

List comprehensions are typically faster than traditional `for` loops for creating lists because they are optimized for that purpose internally. In many cases, the speed difference is negligible for small datasets, but for large datasets, list comprehensions can offer significant performance improvements.

Let's test the speed difference between a `for` loop and a list comprehension for creating a list of squares:

```python
```

```python
import time

# Using a for loop
start_time = time.time()
```

```
squares = []
for i in range(1000000):
    squares.append(i**2)
print("For loop took:", time.time() - start_time)

# Using a list comprehension
start_time = time.time()
squares_comprehension   =   [i**2   for   i   in
range(1000000)]
print("List comprehension took:", time.time() -
start_time)
```

For large numbers, you may observe that the list comprehension is faster than the traditional `for` loop.

---

3. Real-World Example: Processing Data from a CSV File

Let's look at a practical example where we process data from a CSV file using a list comprehension. Suppose you have a CSV file containing information about products in a store, and you want to extract the names of all the products that cost more than $20.

Step 1: Example CSV File

Let's assume you have a CSV file named `products.csv` with the following content:

```
arduino
```

```
Product Name,Price
Laptop,1200
Phone,800
Headphones,50
Mouse,15
Keyboard,30
```

Step 2: Read the CSV File and Use List Comprehension

You can use the `csv` module in Python to read the file and filter the products that cost more than $20.

```python
import csv

# Read the CSV file
with open('products.csv', newline='') as csvfile:
    reader = csv.DictReader(csvfile)

    # Use list comprehension to filter products
with price > 20
    expensive_products = [row['Product Name']
for row in reader if float(row['Price']) > 20]

print(expensive_products)
```

Explanation:

- We use the `csv.DictReader` to read the CSV file, which automatically converts each row into a dictionary where the keys are the column headers (`'Product Name'` and `'Price'`).
- The list comprehension filters out the products that have a price greater than 20.
- The result is a list of product names that cost more than $20.

Output:

```css
['Laptop', 'Phone', 'Headphones', 'Keyboard']
```

4. Conclusion

In this chapter, we've learned:

- **List comprehensions** allow you to create and manipulate lists in a more concise and readable manner.
- List comprehensions improve both the **readability** and **performance** of your code, especially when compared to traditional `for` loops.
- We walked through a real-world example of processing data from a CSV file, demonstrating how list comprehensions can be applied in practical scenarios.

Mastering list comprehensions will not only make your Python code more efficient but also more elegant and Pythonic. In the next chapter, we will dive into **file handling**, where we will explore how to work with files, read and write data, and process large datasets.

CHAPTER 9

INTRODUCTION TO OBJECT-ORIENTED PROGRAMMING

In this chapter, we will explore the fundamentals of **Object-Oriented Programming (OOP)**, which is a programming paradigm that organizes software design around objects and data rather than functions and logic. Python, being an object-oriented language, provides a clear and intuitive way to define and use classes and objects.

We will begin with an overview of **classes** and **objects**, followed by a deep dive into **attributes**, **methods**, and **constructors**. Finally, we will build a real-world example by creating a `Car` class that includes properties like speed, model, and more.

1. Overview of Classes and Objects

1.1 What is a Class?

A **class** in Python is like a blueprint or template for creating objects. It defines the properties (attributes) and behaviors (methods) that the objects created from the class will have. In essence, a class is a user-defined data type that can contain both data and functions.

A class is defined using the `class` keyword followed by the class name. By convention, class names are written in **CamelCase** (i.e., the first letter of each word is capitalized).

Example:

```python
class Car:
    pass  # This is an empty class for now
```

Here, `Car` is the class, and `pass` is a placeholder indicating that the class does nothing yet.

1.2 What is an Object?

An **object** is an instance of a class. While a class defines a structure, an object represents a specific instantiation of that class, with its own unique data.

You can think of a **class** as a blueprint for a house, and an **object** as an actual house built from that blueprint. Multiple houses (objects) can be built from the same blueprint (class), each having different attributes (like color, size, or number of rooms).

Example:

```python
python
```

```python
# Create an object (instance) of the Car class
my_car = Car()
```

In this example, `my_car` is an object of the `Car` class. It will have the properties and behaviors defined by the `Car` class once we define them.

---

2. Attributes, Methods, and Constructors

2.1 Attributes

Attributes (also called properties or fields) are variables that belong to an object or a class. They hold the data about the object. Attributes can be set when creating an object (via the **constructor**) or modified later.

Attributes can be of any data type (strings, integers, lists, etc.) and can be accessed using dot notation (`object.attribute`).

Example:

```python
python

class Car:
    def __init__(self, model, color, speed):
        self.model = model   # Attribute
        self.color = color   # Attribute
        self.speed = speed   # Attribute
```

In the above example:

- `model`, `color`, and `speed` are attributes of the `Car` class.
- The `__init__` method is a special method known as the **constructor**, which initializes the attributes when a new object is created.

2.2 Methods

A **method** is a function that belongs to a class and defines the behaviors of objects created from the class. Methods are used to manipulate the object's data (attributes) or perform actions.

Methods are defined like regular functions but with the first parameter always being `self`, which refers to the instance (object) of the class.

Example:

```python
python

class Car:
    def __init__(self, model, color, speed):
        self.model = model
        self.color = color
        self.speed = speed

    def accelerate(self, increment):
        self.speed += increment
        print(f"The car is now going {self.speed} km/h.")

    def stop(self):
        self.speed = 0
        print("The car has stopped.")
```

In this example:

- The `accelerate()` method increases the speed of the car.
- The `stop()` method sets the car's speed to zero.

2.3 Constructor (the __init__ method)

The **constructor** in Python is the special method __init__(). It is automatically called when a new object is created. This method is used to initialize the attributes of the object with values.

The __init__() method is defined with `self` as the first parameter, followed by any other parameters that are needed to initialize the object's attributes.

Example:

python

```python
class Car:
    def __init__(self, model, color, speed):
        self.model = model
        self.color = color
        self.speed = speed
```

In this example:

- __init__() takes `model`, `color`, and `speed` as parameters and initializes the object's attributes with those values.

3. Real-World Example: Building a Car Class with Properties like Speed, Model, etc.

Let's put our knowledge of classes, attributes, and methods into practice by building a `Car` class. The class will have the following properties:

- **Attributes**: `model, color, speed`
- **Methods**:
    - `accelerate()` to increase the speed of the car.
    - `decelerate()` to decrease the speed of the car.
    - `stop()` to stop the car (set speed to 0).
    - `get_info()` to display the car's information.

Example Code:

python

```python
class Car:
    def __init__(self, model, color, speed=0):
        # Constructor to initialize the car's
model, color, and speed
        self.model = model
        self.color = color
        self.speed = speed

    def accelerate(self, increment):
```

105

```python
        # Increases the car's speed
        self.speed += increment
        print(f"The car is now going {self.speed}
km/h.")


    def decelerate(self, decrement):
        # Decreases the car's speed
        if self.speed - decrement < 0:
            self.speed = 0
        else:
            self.speed -= decrement
        print(f"The car is now going {self.speed}
km/h.")


    def stop(self):
        # Stops the car (sets speed to 0)
        self.speed = 0
        print("The car has stopped.")


    def get_info(self):
        # Displays information about the car
        print(f"Car Model: {self.model}")
        print(f"Car Color: {self.color}")
        print(f"Car Speed: {self.speed} km/h")
```

Explanation:

- **Constructor**: The __init__ () method initializes the car with a model, color, and an optional speed (defaulting to 0).
- **Methods**:
  - accelerate(): Increases the car's speed by a given increment.
  - decelerate(): Decreases the car's speed by a given decrement, ensuring the speed doesn't go below 0.
  - stop(): Sets the speed to 0, effectively stopping the car.
  - get_info(): Displays the current state of the car (model, color, and speed).

Example Usage:

python

```
# Create a new Car object
my_car = Car("Tesla Model S", "Red")

# Display car information
my_car.get_info()
```

```python
# Accelerate the car
my_car.accelerate(50)

# Decelerate the car
my_car.decelerate(20)

# Stop the car
my_car.stop()

# Display car information again
my_car.get_info()
```

Output:

yaml

```
Car Model: Tesla Model S
Car Color: Red
Car Speed: 0 km/h
The car is now going 50 km/h.
The car is now going 30 km/h.
The car has stopped.
Car Model: Tesla Model S
Car Color: Red
Car Speed: 0 km/h
```

4. Conclusion

In this chapter, we:

- Explored the basic principles of **Object-Oriented Programming (OOP)**, including **classes** and **objects**.
- Learned about **attributes**, **methods**, and the **constructor** (`__init__`) in Python.
- Built a **Car class** with methods to accelerate, decelerate, stop, and display car information.

OOP is a powerful paradigm that helps organize code, making it more modular and easier to manage. In the next chapter, we will dive deeper into **inheritance, polymorphism**, and other advanced OOP concepts, which allow you to build even more complex and reusable code.

CHAPTER 10

INHERITANCE: REUSING CODE

In this chapter, we will explore the concept of **inheritance** in Python, which allows us to extend existing classes and reuse code. We'll learn how to create a base class, extend it using inheritance, and override methods for more specific behavior. Additionally, we'll see how to use the `super()` function to call methods from the base class.

We will also go through a real-world example of creating a system for **employees**, where **Managers** inherit from the **Employee** class, demonstrating how inheritance can be used to reduce redundancy and make code more modular.

1. Understanding Inheritance and How to Extend Classes

Inheritance is a mechanism in object-oriented programming that allows a class to inherit attributes and methods from another class. The class that is inherited from is called the **parent class** (or **base class**), and the class that inherits is called the **child class** (or **derived class**).

110

Inheritance allows us to **extend** the functionality of an existing class, making it easier to create new classes without rewriting the same code. The child class can **inherit** the methods and attributes of the parent class and **extend** or **override** them as needed.

1.1 Basic Syntax of Inheritance

The child class is defined by specifying the parent class in parentheses after the class name.

Syntax:

```python

class ChildClass(ParentClass):
    # Child class-specific code
```

- **ParentClass**: The class from which we inherit.
- **ChildClass**: The class that inherits from the parent class.

Example: Creating a `Person` class and a `Student` class that inherits from `Person`.

```python
```

```python
class Person:
    def __init__(self, name, age):
        self.name = name
        self.age = age

    def greet(self):
        print(f"Hello, my name is {self.name} and I am {self.age} years old.")

class Student(Person):
    def __init__(self, name, age, student_id):
        # Inheriting attributes from the Person class
        super().__init__(name, age)
        self.student_id = student_id

    def greet(self):
        # Overriding the greet method to add student-specific info
        print(f"Hello, I am {self.name}, a student with ID {self.student_id}.")

# Create an instance of Student
student = Student("Alice", 20, "S12345")
student.greet()
```

Output:

css

112

```
Hello, I am Alice, a student with ID S12345.
```

In this example:

- `Student` is the child class that inherits from the `Person` parent class.
- The `Student` class calls the constructor of the `Person` class using `super()` and adds a new attribute `student_id`.
- We override the `greet()` method in `Student` to provide specific behavior.

---

2. Overriding Methods and Using `super()`

2.1 Overriding Methods

When a method in the child class has the same name as a method in the parent class, it **overrides** the parent class's method. This allows the child class to modify the behavior of the inherited method.

In the previous example, the `greet()` method was overridden in the `Student` class to provide a more specific greeting for students.

2.2 Using `super()`

The `super()` function is used to call methods from the parent class in the child class. This is helpful when you want to **extend** the functionality of the parent class method but still want to reuse some of the code from the parent class.

Syntax:

python

```
super().method_name(arguments)
```

Example:

python

```
class Person:
    def __init__(self, name, age):
        self.name = name
        self.age = age

    def greet(self):
        print(f"Hello, my name is {self.name} and
I am {self.age} years old.")

class Employee(Person):
    def __init__(self, name, age, position):
```

```
        # Calling the constructor of the parent
class
        super().__init__(name, age)
        self.position = position

    def greet(self):
        # Using super() to call the parent class
greet method
        super().greet()
        print(f"I work as a {self.position}.")

# Create an instance of Employee
employee = Employee("Bob", 35, "Software
Engineer")
employee.greet()
```

Output:

```
pgsql
```

```
Hello, my name is Bob and I am 35 years old.
I work as a Software Engineer.
```

In this example:

- The Employee class inherits from Person.

- The greet() method in Employee uses super().greet() to call the parent class greet()

115

method and then extends it by adding information about the employee's position.

---

3. Real-World Example: Creating a System for Employees where Managers Inherit from Employee

In this example, we will create a simple system for managing employees. We will define an `Employee` class and then extend it by creating a `Manager` class. The `Manager` class will inherit from `Employee` but will have additional responsibilities, such as managing a team of employees.

3.1 Defining the `Employee` Class

The `Employee` class will have basic attributes like `name`, `age`, and `salary`, and a method to display employee information.

3.2 Defining the `Manager` Class

The `Manager` class will inherit from the `Employee` class and will have an additional attribute `team_size` to represent the number of employees a manager oversees. The `Manager` class will also override the `display_info()` method to include information about the manager's team size.

Example Code:

python

```python
class Employee:
    def __init__(self, name, age, salary):
        self.name = name
        self.age = age
        self.salary = salary

    def display_info(self):
        print(f"Employee Name: {self.name}")
        print(f"Age: {self.age}")
        print(f"Salary: ${self.salary}")

class Manager(Employee):
    def __init__(self, name, age, salary, team_size):
        # Inheriting attributes from the Employee class
        super().__init__(name, age, salary)
        self.team_size = team_size

    def display_info(self):
        # Overriding the display_info method to include team size
        super().display_info()
        print(f"Team Size: {self.team_size}")
```

```python
    def assign_task(self, task):
        print(f"Manager {self.name} has assigned
the task: {task}")

# Creating an instance of Employee
employee = Employee("Alice", 28, 50000)
employee.display_info()

print("\n")

# Creating an instance of Manager
manager = Manager("Bob", 40, 80000, 10)
manager.display_info()
manager.assign_task("Complete    the    quarterly
report")
```

Output:

```yaml
yaml

Employee Name: Alice
Age: 28
Salary: $50000

Employee Name: Bob
Age: 40
Salary: $80000
Team Size: 10
```

Manager Bob has assigned the task: Complete the quarterly report

Explanation:

- The `Employee` class has attributes for `name`, `age`, and `salary`, and a method `display_info()` that prints the employee's information.
- The `Manager` class inherits from `Employee` and adds a `team_size` attribute.
- The `display_info()` method in `Manager` calls `super().display_info()` to reuse the code from the `Employee` class and then extends it to display the team size.
- The `Manager` class also has an additional method `assign_task()` that is specific to managers.

---

4. Conclusion

In this chapter, we learned the following key concepts:

- **Inheritance** allows us to create a new class (child) that extends the functionality of an existing class (parent).
- The **child class** can inherit methods and attributes from the **parent class** and can also **override methods** to change their behavior.

119

- We used the **super()** function to call methods from the parent class within the child class.
- We saw a real-world example of using inheritance to model a **Manager** class that inherits from the **Employee** class.

Inheritance is a powerful feature of object-oriented programming that helps reduce redundancy and allows for more flexible and maintainable code. In the next chapter, we will explore other OOP concepts like **polymorphism** and **encapsulation**, which build on inheritance to provide even more flexibility in your code design.

CHAPTER 11

POLYMORPHISM AND ENCAPSULATION

In this chapter, we will dive into two important concepts in object-oriented programming (OOP) in Python: **Polymorphism** and **Encapsulation**. These concepts help make our code more flexible, maintainable, and efficient.

We will begin by explaining **polymorphism**, including **method overriding** and **duck typing**. Then, we'll cover **encapsulation**, including the use of **private** and **public** attributes and methods. Finally, we'll build a real-world example of handling multiple shapes (like `Circle` and `Square`) using polymorphism.

1. Polymorphism: Method Overriding and Duck Typing

Polymorphism means "many shapes" and refers to the ability of different classes to provide a specific implementation of the same method or function. There are two main types of polymorphism in Python:

- **Method Overriding**: When a child class provides its own version of a method that is already defined in the parent class.
- **Duck Typing**: Python's dynamic nature allows objects to be used based on their behavior (methods and properties) rather than their actual type.

1.1 Method Overriding

Method overriding occurs when a subclass defines a method with the same name as a method in its parent class. The child class method **overrides** the parent class method, allowing the child class to provide its own implementation.

Syntax:

```python
class ParentClass:
    def method(self):
        pass  # parent method

class ChildClass(ParentClass):
    def method(self):
        pass  # overridden child method
```

Example: Method Overriding

```python
python

class Animal:
    def speak(self):
        print("Animal makes a sound")

class Dog(Animal):
    def speak(self):
        print("Dog barks")

class Cat(Animal):
    def speak(self):
        print("Cat meows")

# Creating instances
dog = Dog()
cat = Cat()

dog.speak()  # Output: Dog barks
cat.speak()  # Output: Cat meows
```

In this example:

- The `Dog` and `Cat` classes both override the `speak()` method from the `Animal` class, providing their own specific implementations.
- When we call `speak()` on a `Dog` or `Cat` object, the respective overridden method is executed.

1.2 Duck Typing

Duck typing refers to Python's ability to check an object's behavior rather than its actual type. The saying **"If it looks like a duck and quacks like a duck, it's a duck"** captures the essence of duck typing. In Python, this means that you can pass any object to a function as long as it supports the necessary methods or attributes, regardless of the object's actual class.

Example:

python

```python
class Bird:
    def fly(self):
        print("Bird is flying")

class Airplane:
    def fly(self):
        print("Airplane is flying")

def make_it_fly(obj):
    obj.fly()

bird = Bird()
airplane = Airplane()
```

```
make_it_fly(bird)       # Output: Bird is flying
make_it_fly(airplane)   # Output: Airplane is
flying
```

Here, even though `Bird` and `Airplane` are unrelated classes, both implement a `fly()` method. The `make_it_fly()` function doesn't care about the type of the object passed; it only cares if the object has a `fly()` method. This is a classic example of duck typing in action.

---

2. Encapsulation: Private and Public Attributes and Methods

Encapsulation refers to the practice of bundling the data (attributes) and methods that operate on the data into a single unit or class. In Python, encapsulation also involves restricting access to certain attributes and methods to ensure the internal state of an object is protected from outside interference.

In Python, we use **public** and **private** attributes and methods to control access.

2.1 Public Attributes and Methods

By default, all attributes and methods in Python are **public**, meaning they can be accessed from outside the class.

Example:

python

```python
class Car:
    def __init__(self, model, speed):
        self.model = model  # Public attribute
        self.speed = speed  # Public attribute

    def accelerate(self):
        self.speed += 10
        print(f"The car is now going {self.speed}
km/h")

# Creating a Car object
my_car = Car("Tesla", 50)
my_car.accelerate()   # Output: The car is now
going 60 km/h
print(my_car.model)  # Accessing public attribute
directly
```

Here:

- model and speed are public attributes, and accelerate() is a public method.
- We can access and modify the public attributes directly, like my_car.model.

2.2 Private Attributes and Methods

Private attributes and methods are those that are intended to be accessed only within the class. In Python, we denote private attributes and methods by prefixing them with double underscores (__).

Example:

```python
python

class Car:
    def __init__(self, model, speed):
        self.__model = model  # Private attribute
        self.__speed = speed  # Private attribute

    def __accelerate(self):  # Private method
        self.__speed += 10
        print(f"The    car    is    now    going
{self.__speed} km/h")

    def public_accelerate(self):
        self.__accelerate()    # Calling the
private method inside the class

# Creating a Car object
my_car = Car("Tesla", 50)
my_car.public_accelerate()  # Accessing private
method via public method
```

```
# Accessing private attribute and method directly
(will raise an error)
# print(my_car.__model)  # AttributeError: 'Car'
object has no attribute '__model'
```

In this example:

- The attributes __model and __speed are private, as is the method __accelerate().
- You cannot access private attributes or methods directly from outside the class. Attempting to do so will raise an AttributeError.
- The method public_accelerate() is provided as a public interface to access the private method.

To access private attributes from outside the class, you can use Python's **name mangling** (not recommended for general use):

python

```
# Accessing private attribute using name mangling
print(my_car._Car__model)  # This will work but
is not advised
```

3. Real-World Example: A System that Handles Multiple Shapes (Circle, Square) Using Polymorphism

Let's now look at a real-world example where we apply polymorphism to handle different types of shapes (`Circle` and `Square`) in a unified way. Both shapes will inherit from a base class `Shape` and implement their own version of the `area()` method.

3.1 Defining the Shape Base Class

The `Shape` class will serve as the base class with a method `area()`, which will be overridden in the child classes.

Example Code:

```python

import math

class Shape:
    def area(self):
        pass  # This method will be overridden by
subclasses

class Circle(Shape):
    def __init__(self, radius):
```

```python
        self.radius = radius

    def area(self):
        return math.pi * self.radius ** 2    #
Formula for the area of a circle

class Square(Shape):
    def __init__(self, side_length):
        self.side_length = side_length

    def area(self):
        return self.side_length ** 2   # Formula
for the area of a square

# Creating objects of Circle and Square
circle = Circle(5)
square = Square(4)

# Polymorphism: Calling the same method on
different objects
shapes = [circle, square]
for shape in shapes:
    print(f"Area: {shape.area()}")   # The correct
area method is called for each shape
```

Output:

```
makefile
```

```
Area: 78.53981633974483
```

```
Area: 16
```

Explanation:

- The `Shape` class is the **base class** with a placeholder `area()` method.
- The `Circle` and `Square` classes **inherit** from the `Shape` class and override the `area()` method to provide their own implementation.
- We create instances of `Circle` and `Square`, then loop through them and call `area()` polymorphically. Even though both objects are instances of different classes, the correct `area()` method is called for each object based on its type.

---

4. Conclusion

In this chapter, we covered:

- **Polymorphism**, including **method overriding** and **duck typing** in Python, which allows objects to behave differently based on their class while using the same interface.
- **Encapsulation**, including how to define **private** and **public** attributes and methods to control access to the internal state of an object.

- A **real-world example** where we created a system that handles multiple shapes (`Circle` and `Square`) using polymorphism, demonstrating how to design flexible systems.

Polymorphism and encapsulation are powerful OOP concepts that allow you to write more reusable, maintainable, and flexible code. In the next chapter, we will explore **abstract classes** and **interfaces** to understand how to design systems with a clear blueprint for future development.

CHAPTER 12

ADVANCED OOP CONCEPTS: ABSTRACTION AND INTERFACES

In this chapter, we will explore two advanced concepts of Object-Oriented Programming (OOP): **Abstraction** and **Interfaces**. These concepts allow you to design more flexible and modular systems by hiding unnecessary implementation details and defining clear structures for interacting with objects.

We'll dive into **Abstraction**, its importance in reducing complexity, and how Python achieves abstraction through **abstract base classes (ABCs)**. Additionally, we'll create a **plugin system** that utilizes interfaces to ensure consistency across various plugins.

---

1. Abstraction: Hiding Implementation Details

Abstraction refers to the concept of hiding the implementation details of an object and exposing only the essential features or behaviors. This simplifies interaction with complex systems by allowing users to focus on high-level functionalities rather than the intricate workings underneath.

133

In Python, abstraction is typically achieved using **abstract base classes (ABCs)**, which define abstract methods that must be implemented by any subclass.

1.1 Why Use Abstraction?

Abstraction helps in the following ways:

- **Simplifies code**: By hiding unnecessary details, you make your code easier to read and understand.
- **Improves maintainability**: It reduces the need to modify multiple parts of your codebase when making changes to the internal implementation.
- **Encourages modularity**: Each class can focus on its specific responsibilities without worrying about the implementation details of others.

1.2 How Abstraction Works in Python

Python supports abstraction through the **abc module**. The abc module provides the **ABC** class and the **@abstractmethod** decorator to define abstract base classes and enforce the implementation of abstract methods.

Syntax:

```python
from abc import ABC, abstractmethod

class MyAbstractClass(ABC):
    @abstractmethod
    def my_method(self):
        pass
```

In the above example:

- **ABC** is the base class for defining abstract base classes.
- **@abstractmethod** is a decorator that marks methods as abstract. These methods must be implemented in any subclass of the abstract class.

1.3 Abstract Base Classes (ABCs)

An **abstract base class** defines a blueprint for other classes. It may contain both abstract methods (which must be overridden) and concrete methods (which can have implementations). Abstract classes cannot be instantiated directly; they can only be used as a base for other classes.

Example of Abstract Base Class:

python

```python
from abc import ABC, abstractmethod

class Shape(ABC):
    @abstractmethod
    def area(self):
        pass

    @abstractmethod
    def perimeter(self):
        pass

class Circle(Shape):
    def __init__(self, radius):
        self.radius = radius

    def area(self):
        return 3.14 * self.radius ** 2

    def perimeter(self):
        return 2 * 3.14 * self.radius

class Rectangle(Shape):
    def __init__(self, length, width):
        self.length = length
        self.width = width
```

```python
    def area(self):
        return self.length * self.width

    def perimeter(self):
        return 2 * (self.length + self.width)

# Create instances of Circle and Rectangle
circle = Circle(5)
print(f"Circle Area: {circle.area()}, Perimeter:
{circle.perimeter()}")

rectangle = Rectangle(4, 6)
print(f"Rectangle    Area:    {rectangle.area()},
Perimeter: {rectangle.perimeter()}")
```

Output:

```
mathematica

Circle Area: 78.5, Perimeter: 31.400000000000002
Rectangle Area: 24, Perimeter: 20
```

In this example:

- Shape is an abstract base class with abstract methods
  area() and perimeter().
- Both Circle and Rectangle are concrete subclasses
  that implement the abstract methods.

- We cannot create an instance of `Shape` directly because it contains abstract methods, but we can create instances of `Circle` and `Rectangle`, which implement all the abstract methods.

---

2. Python Abstract Base Classes (ABCs)

Python's **abc** module enables us to define abstract base classes and enforce abstraction within our code. This ensures that subclasses adhere to a specific interface or behavior, reducing the risk of errors and promoting a clean design.

2.1 Defining Abstract Methods

Abstract methods are methods that have no implementation in the base class but must be implemented by any derived class.

Example:

```python
python

from abc import ABC, abstractmethod

class Animal(ABC):
    @abstractmethod
    def sound(self):
```

```
        pass

class Dog(Animal):
    def sound(self):
        print("Bark")

class Cat(Animal):
    def sound(self):
        print("Meow")

# Instantiate Dog and Cat
dog = Dog()
dog.sound()   # Output: Bark

cat = Cat()
cat.sound()   # Output: Meow
```

In this example:

- `sound()` is an abstract method in the `Animal` class that must be implemented by any subclass.
- Both `Dog` and `Cat` classes provide their own implementations of the `sound()` method.

2.2 Enforcing Interface Consistency

Using abstract classes ensures that subclasses maintain a consistent interface, making it easier to interact with them polymorphically.

For example, regardless of whether we have a `Dog` or a `Cat`, we know both classes will have a `sound()` method, and we can call it in a consistent way.

---

3. Real-World Example: Designing a Plugin System Where Plugins Implement a Common Interface

Let's apply abstraction and interfaces by designing a **plugin system**. In this system, we will define a base class `Plugin` with an abstract method `execute()`. Plugins will implement this interface by defining their own `execute()` method. This will allow us to create different types of plugins that share a common interface and behavior.

3.1 Defining the Plugin Base Class

The `Plugin` class will be an abstract base class with an abstract method `execute()`. Each plugin will implement this method.

Example Code:

```python
from abc import ABC, abstractmethod

class Plugin(ABC):
    @abstractmethod
    def execute(self):
        pass

class LoggingPlugin(Plugin):
    def execute(self):
        print("Logging data...")

class NotificationPlugin(Plugin):
    def execute(self):
        print("Sending notifications...")

class DataProcessingPlugin(Plugin):
    def execute(self):
        print("Processing data...")

# Create a list of plugins
plugins = [LoggingPlugin(), NotificationPlugin(), DataProcessingPlugin()]

# Execute each plugin
for plugin in plugins:
    plugin.execute()
```

Output:

```kotlin
Logging data...
Sending notifications...
Processing data...
```

Explanation:

- The `Plugin` class is an abstract base class with an abstract `execute()` method.
- The `LoggingPlugin`, `NotificationPlugin`, and `DataProcessingPlugin` classes each provide their own implementation of the `execute()` method.
- The `plugins` list stores instances of the different plugin types.
- The `for` loop iterates over the list of plugins and calls their `execute()` method. Each plugin behaves according to its own implementation.

This is a simple plugin system where we can add new plugins by subclassing the `Plugin` class and implementing the `execute()` method.

4. Conclusion

In this chapter, we explored:

- **Abstraction**: We learned how to hide the implementation details of a class using abstract base classes (ABCs) and abstract methods. This allows us to focus on the essential behaviors of objects while hiding unnecessary details.

- **Python's abstract base classes**: We used the `abc` module to enforce abstraction in Python, ensuring that subclasses implement required methods.

- **Real-world example**: We built a plugin system where plugins implement a common interface, demonstrating how abstraction and interfaces can be used to create modular and extensible systems.

Abstraction and interfaces are key principles in OOP that help create flexible and maintainable systems. In the next chapter, we will explore **decorators** and **property decorators** to manage class behaviors and attributes in a more sophisticated way.

CHAPTER 13

WORKING WITH DATA STRUCTURES IN DEPTH

In this chapter, we will take a **deep dive** into Python's fundamental data structures: **lists**, **tuples**, **dictionaries**, and **sets**. These data structures are crucial for organizing and manipulating data in Python programs. Understanding their strengths, weaknesses, and when to use them is essential for writing efficient, clean code.

We'll also apply these concepts to build a **real-world to-do list application** that demonstrates the practical usage of these data structures.

1. Deep Dive into Lists, Tuples, Dictionaries, and Sets

1.1 Lists

A **list** is one of the most commonly used data structures in Python. Lists are **ordered** collections of items that can be of different types. They are **mutable**, meaning that you can modify the contents of a list after its creation.

Key Characteristics:

- **Ordered**: The items in a list have a specific order and can be accessed using an index.
- **Mutable**: You can modify, add, or remove items from a list.
- **Duplicates**: Lists can contain duplicate items.

Example:

python

```
fruits = ["apple", "banana", "cherry", "apple"]
print(fruits[0])   # Output: apple
fruits.append("orange")   # Adds 'orange' to the
end of the list
print(fruits)    # Output: ['apple', 'banana',
'cherry', 'apple', 'orange']
```

When to use lists:

- Use lists when the order of items matters.
- Lists are ideal when you need to store a collection of items and might need to modify them later (e.g., adding or removing elements).

1.2 Tuples

A **tuple** is similar to a list, but it is **immutable**, meaning that once a tuple is created, its contents cannot be changed. Tuples are also **ordered**, and they can contain duplicate values. However, since they are immutable, they are generally faster than lists when you need to store data that shouldn't be modified.

Key Characteristics:

- **Ordered**: The items in a tuple have a specific order, and each item can be accessed using an index.
- **Immutable**: Once a tuple is created, it cannot be changed (no modifying, adding, or removing elements).
- **Duplicates**: Tuples can contain duplicate items.

Example:

python

```
coordinates = (10, 20, 30)
print(coordinates[0])  # Output: 10
# coordinates[1] = 25   # This will raise a
TypeError because tuples are immutable
```

When to use tuples:

- Use tuples when you need an immutable, ordered collection of items.
- They are useful for storing fixed collections of data (e.g., coordinates, days of the week).

1.3 Dictionaries

A **dictionary** is an unordered collection of key-value pairs. Each key is unique, and the value associated with a key can be of any data type. Dictionaries are **mutable**, meaning you can change the values of existing keys or add new key-value pairs.

Key Characteristics:

- **Unordered**: Dictionaries do not maintain the order of items (though Python 3.7+ guarantees insertion order).
- **Mutable**: You can modify, add, or remove key-value pairs.
- **Unique Keys**: Keys in a dictionary must be unique (no duplicate keys), but values can be duplicated.

Example:

python

```
student = {"name": "Alice", "age": 20, "major":
"Computer Science"}
```

147

```
print(student["name"])   # Output: Alice
student["age"] = 21   # Modifying the value of
'age'
student["year"] = 2023  # Adding a new key-value
pair
print(student)   # Output: {'name': 'Alice',
'age': 21, 'major': 'Computer Science', 'year':
2023}
```

When to use dictionaries:

- Use dictionaries when you need to store data in key-value pairs.
- Dictionaries are perfect for scenarios where you need fast lookups by key, such as storing user profiles or mapping product IDs to product details.

1.4 Sets

A **set** is an unordered collection of unique items. Sets are **mutable**, and they are commonly used for eliminating duplicates or performing mathematical set operations like union, intersection, and difference.

Key Characteristics:

- **Unordered**: The items in a set do not have a specific order.
- **Mutable**: You can add and remove elements from a set.
- **Unique Elements**: Sets automatically discard duplicate items.

Example:

python

```
fruits = {"apple", "banana", "cherry", "apple"}
print(fruits)   # Output: {'banana', 'cherry',
'apple'}
fruits.add("orange")  # Adding an item
print(fruits)   # Output: {'banana', 'cherry',
'apple', 'orange'}
fruits.remove("banana")  # Removing an item
print(fruits)   # Output: {'cherry', 'apple',
'orange'}
```

When to use sets:

- Use sets when you need to store a collection of unique items, and order doesn't matter.
- Sets are ideal for performing set operations like union, intersection, and difference, such as comparing two groups of items.

2. When to Use Each Data Structure

Here's a quick guide to when you should choose one data structure over another:

- **Lists**: Use when you need an ordered collection of items, and you might need to modify the data (e.g., adding or removing items).
- **Tuples**: Use when the collection of items should remain constant (immutable), and you don't need to modify the data.
- **Dictionaries**: Use when you need to store key-value pairs, perform fast lookups, or represent data in a mapping relationship.
- **Sets**: Use when you need to store unique items and perform set operations, like finding the intersection or union of two sets.

---

3. Real-World Example: Implementing a To-Do List Application

Now that we have a clear understanding of the data structures, let's implement a **simple to-do list application** using a combination of **lists, tuples**, and **dictionaries**. The to-do list will allow users to add tasks, mark them as completed, and view all tasks.

3.1 Designing the To-Do List

- We will use a **list** to store tasks, where each task will be represented by a **tuple** with the task description and a boolean indicating whether it's completed.
- We will use a **dictionary** to store the user's to-do list, with task IDs as keys and task details as values.

Example Code:

python

```python
class TodoList:
    def __init__(self):
        self.tasks = {}
        self.task_id = 1

    def add_task(self, description):
        task = (description, False)   # Task is
initially not completed
        self.tasks[self.task_id] = task
        print(f"Task {self.task_id} added.")
        self.task_id += 1

    def mark_completed(self, task_id):
```

151

```python
        if task_id in self.tasks:
            description, _ = self.tasks[task_id]
            self.tasks[task_id] = (description,
True)
            print(f"Task {task_id} marked as
completed.")
        else:
            print(f"Task {task_id} not found.")

    def view_tasks(self):
        if not self.tasks:
            print("No tasks to show.")
            return

        for task_id, (description, completed) in
self.tasks.items():
            status = "Completed" if completed
else "Pending"
            print(f"Task            {task_id}:
{description} - {status}")

# Example Usage:
todo_list = TodoList()
todo_list.add_task("Buy groceries")
todo_list.add_task("Complete Python project")
todo_list.view_tasks()

todo_list.mark_completed(1)
todo_list.view_tasks()
```

Output:

```
arduino

Task 1 added.
Task 2 added.
Task 1: Buy groceries - Pending
Task 2: Complete Python project - Pending
Task 1 marked as completed.
Task 1: Buy groceries - Completed
Task 2: Complete Python project - Pending
```

Explanation:

- The `TodoList` class manages tasks using a **dictionary** where each task is associated with a unique `task_id`.
- Each task is stored as a **tuple** containing the task description and a boolean representing the completion status.
- The `add_task()` method adds new tasks to the list.
- The `mark_completed()` method updates the task's status to `True` if the task is found.
- The `view_tasks()` method prints all tasks with their status (either "Pending" or "Completed").

153

4. Conclusion

In this chapter, we:

- Deep-dived into Python's core data structures: **lists**, **tuples**, **dictionaries**, and **sets**, and discussed when to use each of them based on their characteristics.
- We implemented a real-world **to-do list application**, utilizing these data structures to manage tasks efficiently.
- Learned how to leverage the flexibility of data structures to design more practical and efficient applications.

Understanding and using the right data structure is key to building efficient and maintainable programs. In the next chapter, we will dive into **file handling** and learn how to read from and write to files, which is essential for data persistence in applications.

CHAPTER 14

FILE HANDLING: READING AND WRITING FILES

In this chapter, we will explore how to interact with files in Python, including reading and writing text files, CSV files, and more complex formats such as JSON and XML. File handling is an essential skill for most real-world applications, as it allows you to persist data and process external data sources.

We will also work through a **real-world example** involving **log file analysis**, which demonstrates how to read from and parse log files.

1. Opening, Reading, and Writing to Text Files

Python provides built-in functions to handle text files. The most common operation is to open a file, read its contents, and write new data to it. The open() function is used to open a file, and it supports various modes like 'r' for reading, 'w' for writing, and 'a' for appending.

1.1 Opening a File

The `open()` function opens a file and returns a file object. Here's how to open a file:

```python
```

```python
file = open('example.txt', 'r')   # Open the file
in read mode
```

Common modes for opening files:

- `'r'`: Read (default). Opens the file for reading.
- `'w'`: Write. Opens the file for writing (creates the file if it doesn't exist, and truncates it if it does).
- `'a'`: Append. Opens the file for writing (creates the file if it doesn't exist, and appends data to it).
- `'b'`: Binary. Used to open files in binary mode.

1.2 Reading from Files

Once the file is opened, we can read its contents. The following methods are used for reading from files:

- `read()`: Reads the entire file as a string.
- `readline()`: Reads one line from the file.
- `readlines()`: Reads all lines of a file into a list.

156

Example: Reading the Entire File

```python
python
```

```python
with open('example.txt', 'r') as file:
    content = file.read()   # Reads the entire
file
    print(content)
```

Example: Reading Line by Line

```python
python
```

```python
with open('example.txt', 'r') as file:
    for line in file:
        print(line.strip())  # Strips the newline
character
```

1.3 Writing to Files

To write to a file, you can open the file in 'w' or 'a' mode. Writing will overwrite the file in 'w' mode or append new content in 'a' mode.

Example: Writing to a File

```python
python
```

```python
with open('output.txt', 'w') as file:
```

```
file.write("Hello, world!\n")
file.write("This is a new line.")
```

Example: Appending to a File

python

```
with open('output.txt', 'a') as file:
    file.write("\nAppended text.")
```

Using `with` ensures that the file is properly closed after the operations are complete, even if an error occurs.

---

2. Working with CSV Files

CSV (Comma Separated Values) files are widely used for storing tabular data. Python has a built-in `csv` module that makes reading and writing CSV files simple.

2.1 Reading CSV Files

The `csv.reader` is used to read data from a CSV file. Each row is returned as a list of values.

Example: Reading a CSV File

```
python

import csv

with open('data.csv', 'r') as file:
    reader = csv.reader(file)
    for row in reader:
        print(row)  # Each row is a list of values
```

Example: Reading a CSV File into a Dictionary

```
python

import csv

with open('data.csv', 'r') as file:
    reader = csv.DictReader(file)
    for row in reader:
        print(row)   # Each row is a dictionary
where the keys are the column headers
```

2.2 Writing to CSV Files

The csv.writer is used to write data to a CSV file. You can write rows as lists or dictionaries.

Example: Writing to a CSV File

```
python
```

```
import csv

data = [["name", "age", "city"],
        ["Alice", 30, "New York"],
        ["Bob", 25, "Los Angeles"]]

with open('output.csv', 'w', newline='') as file:
    writer = csv.writer(file)
    writer.writerows(data)    # Writing multiple
rows at once
```

Example: Writing a Dictionary to CSV

```
python

import csv

data = [{"name": "Alice", "age": 30, "city": "New
York"},
        {"name": "Bob", "age": 25, "city": "Los
Angeles"}]

with open('output.csv', 'w', newline='') as file:
    fieldnames = ["name", "age", "city"]
    writer          =         csv.DictWriter(file,
fieldnames=fieldnames)
    writer.writeheader()   # Writing the header
row
    writer.writerows(data)   # Writing the data
```

160

3. Working with JSON and XML Files

JSON (JavaScript Object Notation) and XML (Extensible Markup Language) are popular formats for storing and exchanging structured data.

3.1 Working with JSON Files

Python provides the `json` module for parsing and writing JSON data. JSON is widely used for API responses, configuration files, and other data formats.

Example: Reading from a JSON File

```python
python

import json

with open('data.json', 'r') as file:
    data = json.load(file)  # Loads the JSON data
into a Python dictionary
    print(data)
```

Example: Writing to a JSON File

```python
python
```

161

```
import json

data = {"name": "Alice", "age": 30, "city": "New
York"}

with open('output.json', 'w') as file:
    json.dump(data, file, indent=4)   # Writes
data to the file with indentation
```

3.2 Working with XML Files

For XML files, Python provides the `xml.etree.ElementTree` module, which allows you to parse and create XML documents.

Example: Parsing XML

```python
python

import xml.etree.ElementTree as ET

tree = ET.parse('data.xml')
root = tree.getroot()

for child in root:
    print(child.tag, child.attrib)
```

Example: Writing to XML

```
python

import xml.etree.ElementTree as ET

root = ET.Element("data")
child1 = ET.SubElement(root, "item")
child1.text = "Item 1"

tree = ET.ElementTree(root)
tree.write("output.xml")
```

---

4. Real-World Example: Log File Analysis and Parsing

Let's now apply these file handling techniques to a **real-world example**: parsing and analyzing a log file. We'll use a log file that contains multiple entries with timestamps, log levels, and messages.

4.1 Sample Log File

Assume we have a log file (`logs.txt`) with the following content:

```
pgsql

2022-09-01 12:30:45 INFO User logged in
```

```
2022-09-01 12:35:10 ERROR Failed to connect to
database
2022-09-01 12:40:05 WARNING Low disk space
2022-09-01 12:45:30 INFO User logged out
```

We want to:

- Read the log file.
- Filter the log entries by log level (e.g., ERROR).
- Store the filtered logs in a separate file.

4.2 Parsing the Log File

python

```python
def parse_log(file_path, log_level="ERROR"):
    with open(file_path, 'r') as file:
        logs = file.readlines()

    filtered_logs = [log for log in logs if
log.startswith(log_level)]

    return filtered_logs

def write_filtered_logs(logs, output_path):
    with open(output_path, 'w') as file:
        file.writelines(logs)
```

```
# Example Usage
log_file_path = 'logs.txt'
filtered_logs    =    parse_log(log_file_path,
log_level="ERROR")
write_filtered_logs(filtered_logs,
'error_logs.txt')

print("Filtered    logs    written    to
'error_logs.txt'.")
```

Explanation:

- We define a function `parse_log()` that reads the log file and filters the entries based on the `log_level` (e.g., ERROR).
- The `write_filtered_logs()` function writes the filtered logs to a new file.
- We call these functions to parse the `logs.txt` file, filter the ERROR logs, and save them to `error_logs.txt`.

---

5. Conclusion

In this chapter, we learned:

- How to **read** and **write** text files, CSV files, JSON files, and XML files in Python using built-in modules.

- The key differences between these file formats and when to use each.

- A **real-world example** of log file analysis, where we parsed a log file, filtered entries by log level, and saved the results to a new file.

File handling is essential for data persistence and interacting with external data sources. In the next chapter, we will delve into **data manipulation** and explore libraries like **Pandas** to handle structured data more efficiently.

CHAPTER 15

HANDLING EXTERNAL DATA WITH APIS

In this chapter, we will explore how to handle external data in Python using **APIs** (Application Programming Interfaces). We will specifically focus on **RESTful APIs**, which are the most common type of API used in web services. We'll also look at how to fetch data from an API using the popular `requests` library. To illustrate these concepts, we will build a **real-world example** where we fetch **weather data** from an API.

1. Introduction to RESTful APIs

APIs allow different software systems to communicate with each other. A **RESTful API** (Representational State Transfer) is a web service that follows a set of architectural principles to allow access to resources (data) over the web. RESTful APIs use standard HTTP methods, such as `GET`, `POST`, `PUT`, and `DELETE`, to perform operations on resources.

1.1 Key Concepts in RESTful APIs

- **Resources**: In a RESTful API, resources (such as data entities) are identified by URLs. For example, `/users` could represent a list of users, while `/users/1` represents a specific user with ID 1.
- **HTTP Methods**: REST APIs use the following HTTP methods:
  - **GET**: Retrieves data from the server.
  - **POST**: Sends data to the server to create a new resource.
  - **PUT**: Updates an existing resource on the server.
  - **DELETE**: Deletes a resource from the server.
- **JSON**: Most RESTful APIs exchange data in **JSON** format because it is lightweight and easy to work with.

1.2 Anatomy of a RESTful API Request

A typical RESTful API request includes:

1. **Endpoint URL**: The URL where the API resource is located.
2. **HTTP Method**: The operation we want to perform (e.g., `GET`).
3. **Headers**: Optional metadata about the request, such as authentication tokens.

4. **Parameters**: Query parameters (for GET requests) or data (for POST, PUT requests).

For example:

```bash
bash
```

```
GET
https://api.openweathermap.org/data/2.5/weather
?q=London&appid=your_api_key
```

In this example:

- **Endpoint**: /data/2.5/weather
- **Query Parameters**: q=London (city name) and appid=your_api_key (API key for authentication)

---

2. Fetching Data Using the requests Library

Python's requests library makes it easy to send HTTP requests and handle API responses. The requests module provides functions for sending **GET, POST, PUT,** and **DELETE** requests, as well as handling responses in various formats (e.g., JSON, text).

2.1 Installing requests

First, ensure that the `requests` library is installed. You can install it using `pip`:

```bash
bash
```

```bash
pip install requests
```

2.2 Making a Simple GET Request

To interact with a RESTful API, the most common operation is to send a **GET request** to fetch data.

Example: Fetching data from a public API:

```python
python
```

```python
import requests

url                                       =
"https://jsonplaceholder.typicode.com/posts"
response = requests.get(url)

# Check if the request was successful
if response.status_code == 200:
    data  =  response.json()    # Convert the
response to JSON format
    print(data)
else:
```

```
print(f"Failed to retrieve data. Status code:
{response.status_code}")
```

In this example:

- `requests.get(url)` sends a GET request to the specified URL.
- `response.status_code` checks if the request was successful (200 OK).
- `response.json()` converts the response body into a Python dictionary.

2.3 Handling Query Parameters

Many APIs require query parameters to filter or modify the data returned. You can pass query parameters using the `params` argument in the `requests.get()` method.

Example: Fetching posts by a specific user:

```python

import requests

url                                            =
"https://jsonplaceholder.typicode.com/posts"
params = {"userId": 1}
```

```
response = requests.get(url, params=params)

if response.status_code == 200:
    data = response.json()
    print(data)
else:
    print(f"Failed to retrieve data. Status code:
{response.status_code}")
```

Here, we pass a query parameter `userId=1` to retrieve posts by the user with ID 1.

---

3. Real-World Example: Fetching Weather Data from an API

Now let's build a practical example where we fetch **weather data** from a real API: **OpenWeatherMap**. OpenWeatherMap provides free access to weather data through its RESTful API.

3.1 Registering for an API Key

To use the OpenWeatherMap API, you'll need to create a free account and obtain an API key:

1. Go to OpenWeatherMap.
2. Register and get your free API key.

3.2 Fetching Weather Data

Let's write a Python program to fetch the current weather for a specific city (e.g., **London**) using the OpenWeatherMap API.

python

```python
import requests

# Your OpenWeatherMap API key
api_key = "your_api_key_here"

# Base URL for the OpenWeatherMap API
base_url = "https://api.openweathermap.org/data/2.5/weather"

# City for which you want to get the weather
city = "London"

# Complete URL with query parameters
url = f"{base_url}?q={city}&appid={api_key}&units=metric"

# Send the GET request
response = requests.get(url)

# Check if the request was successful
```

173

```
if response.status_code == 200:
    data = response.json()    # Convert the
response to JSON format
    main = data['main']    # Extract the main
weather data
    weather = data['weather'][0]    # Extract
weather condition

    # Print the results
    print(f"Weather in {city}:")
    print(f"Temperature: {main['temp']}°C")
    print(f"Humidity: {main['humidity']}%")
    print(f"Weather: {weather['description']}")
else:
    print(f"Failed to retrieve data. Status code:
{response.status_code}")
```

Explanation:

- **API URL**: The base URL for the OpenWeatherMap API is
  https://api.openweathermap.org/data/2.5/w
  eather.
- We append the city name (q=London), the API key
  (appid=your_api_key_here), and the units
  (units=metric) to the URL.

- **Response Handling**: If the request is successful, the response is converted to JSON, and we extract and print the temperature, humidity, and weather description.

Example Output:

```yaml

Weather in London:
Temperature: 18.5°C
Humidity: 82%
Weather: scattered clouds
```

4. Conclusion

In this chapter, we:

- Introduced **RESTful APIs** and discussed how they allow different software systems to interact with each other over the web.
- Learned how to use the **requests library** to send HTTP requests, handle responses, and work with query parameters.
- Built a **real-world example** that demonstrates how to fetch weather data from the OpenWeatherMap API, process it, and display the results.

Handling external data via APIs is a fundamental skill when working with web applications, external data sources, or third-party services. In the next chapter, we will explore **web scraping** to extract data from websites when APIs are not available.

CHAPTER 16

WORKING WITH DATABASES

In this chapter, we will explore how to interact with databases in Python. Databases are essential for storing and managing data in modern applications. We will introduce **SQL** and **NoSQL** databases, explain how to connect Python to databases using popular libraries, and build a **real-world example**: a **contact manager** that stores data in an **SQLite** database.

1. Introduction to SQL and NoSQL Databases

Databases are categorized into two major types: **SQL (Structured Query Language)** databases and **NoSQL (Not Only SQL)** databases. Each type is suited for different types of data and application needs.

1.1 SQL Databases

SQL databases are relational databases that use structured query language (SQL) for defining and managing the data. They are best suited for applications where the data has a clear structure and relationships between entities. SQL databases are based on tables with rows and columns.

- **Popular SQL databases**: MySQL, PostgreSQL, SQLite, Microsoft SQL Server, Oracle.
- **Characteristics**:
  - **Structured data**: The data is organized into tables with predefined schemas.
  - **ACID compliant**: SQL databases are known for their reliability and support for ACID (Atomicity, Consistency, Isolation, Durability) transactions.
  - **Examples**: Relational data models (e.g., a customer table, orders table with foreign keys).

1.2 NoSQL Databases

NoSQL databases are non-relational databases that are designed to handle large volumes of unstructured or semi-structured data. They are ideal for applications with dynamic or flexible schemas, such as storing JSON-like documents.

- **Popular NoSQL databases**: MongoDB, CouchDB, Cassandra, Redis, Firebase.
- **Characteristics**:

o **Unstructured data**: NoSQL databases can store data in various formats (documents, key-value pairs, graphs, etc.).

o **Scalability**: NoSQL databases are horizontally scalable, making them suitable for big data applications.

o **Examples**: JSON documents (e.g., MongoDB), key-value stores (e.g., Redis).

---

2. Connecting Python to Databases

Python provides several libraries and modules to interact with both SQL and NoSQL databases. Let's explore how to connect Python to three popular databases: **SQLite**, **MySQL**, and **MongoDB**.

2.1 Connecting Python to SQLite

SQLite is a lightweight, serverless, self-contained SQL database. It is a great choice for smaller applications or when you need a simple file-based database.

- **Library**: The `sqlite3` library comes built-in with Python and allows interaction with SQLite databases.

Example: Connecting to SQLite

```python
python

import sqlite3

# Connect to SQLite database (it will create the
database file if it doesn't exist)
conn = sqlite3.connect('contacts.db')

# Create a cursor object to execute SQL queries
cursor = conn.cursor()

# Create a table for storing contacts
cursor.execute('''CREATE TABLE IF NOT EXISTS
contacts
                (id INTEGER PRIMARY KEY, name
TEXT, phone TEXT, email TEXT)''')

# Commit changes and close the connection
conn.commit()
conn.close()
```

In this example:

- We use `sqlite3.connect('contacts.db')` to create or connect to the `contacts.db` SQLite database.
- We create a `contacts` table with columns for `id`, `name`, `phone`, and `email`.

2.2 Connecting Python to MySQL

MySQL is a popular relational database management system. To connect Python to MySQL, we need the `mysql-connector-python` library.

- **Library**: Install it using `pip install mysql-connector-python`.

Example: Connecting to MySQL

```python
import mysql.connector

# Establish connection to MySQL
conn = mysql.connector.connect(
    host="localhost",
    user="your_user",
    password="your_password",
    database="your_database"
)

# Create a cursor object to execute queries
cursor = conn.cursor()
```

```
# Example query: Fetch all records from the
"contacts" table
cursor.execute("SELECT * FROM contacts")
for row in cursor.fetchall():
    print(row)

# Close the connection
cursor.close()
conn.close()
```

In this example:

- We use `mysql.connector.connect()` to connect to a MySQL database by providing the necessary connection details like `host`, `user`, `password`, and `database`.
- We execute a query to retrieve all records from the `contacts` table.

2.3 Connecting Python to MongoDB

MongoDB is a NoSQL document-oriented database that stores data in flexible, JSON-like documents. It is widely used for applications requiring horizontal scalability.

- **Library**: Install it using `pip install pymongo`.

Example: Connecting to MongoDB

```python
python

from pymongo import MongoClient

# Connect to MongoDB (default URI is
localhost:27017)
client                                  =
MongoClient("mongodb://localhost:27017/")

# Access a database and collection
db = client['contact_manager']
collection = db['contacts']

# Insert a contact into the collection
contact   =   {"name":   "Alice",   "phone":
"1234567890", "email": "alice@example.com"}
collection.insert_one(contact)

# Fetch and print all contacts
for contact in collection.find():
    print(contact)
```

In this example:

- We use `MongoClient()` to connect to MongoDB.
- We insert a contact into the `contacts` collection and retrieve all records using the `find()` method.

3. Real-World Example: Building a Contact Manager that Stores Data in SQLite

Now let's put our knowledge of databases to use by creating a simple **contact manager** that stores and retrieves contact information (name, phone, email) in an **SQLite** database.

We will implement the following features:

1. Add a new contact.
2. View all contacts.
3. Search for a contact by name.

Example Code: Contact Manager

python

```python
import sqlite3

class ContactManager:
    def __init__(self, db_name='contacts.db'):
        # Connect to the SQLite database
        self.conn = sqlite3.connect(db_name)
        self.cursor = self.conn.cursor()
        self.create_table()

    def create_table(self):
```

```
        # Create the contacts table if it doesn't
exist
        self.cursor.execute('''CREATE   TABLE   IF
NOT EXISTS contacts
                            (id          INTEGER
PRIMARY  KEY,  name  TEXT,  phone  TEXT,  email
TEXT)''')
        self.conn.commit()

    def add_contact(self, name, phone, email):
        # Insert a new contact into the database
        self.cursor.execute("INSERT        INTO
contacts (name, phone, email) VALUES (?, ?, ?)",
                            (name,          phone,
email))
        self.conn.commit()
        print(f"Contact        {name}        added
successfully!")

    def view_contacts(self):
        # Fetch all contacts from the database
        self.cursor.execute("SELECT   *   FROM
contacts")
        contacts = self.cursor.fetchall()
        for contact in contacts:
            print(contact)

    def search_contact(self, name):
        # Search for a contact by name
```

185

```python
        self.cursor.execute("SELECT    *    FROM
contacts WHERE name LIKE ?", ('%' + name + '%',))
        contacts = self.cursor.fetchall()
        if contacts:
            for contact in contacts:
                print(contact)
        else:
            print(f"No contacts found with the
name {name}")


    def close(self):
        # Close the database connection
        self.cursor.close()
        self.conn.close()


# Example Usage
manager = ContactManager()

# Add some contacts
manager.add_contact("Alice",        "1234567890",
"alice@example.com")
manager.add_contact("Bob",        "0987654321",
"bob@example.com")

# View all contacts
print("\nAll Contacts:")
manager.view_contacts()

# Search for a contact
```

```
print("\nSearch for 'Alice':")
manager.search_contact("Alice")

# Close the connection
manager.close()
```

Explanation:

- **ContactManager class**: This class manages the contacts in the SQLite database. It provides methods to add contacts, view contacts, and search for contacts by name.
- **add_contact()**: Adds a new contact to the database.
- **view_contacts()**: Fetches and prints all contacts.
- **search_contact()**: Searches for a contact by name using SQL LIKE.
- **Database operations**: We use SQLite's execute() method to run SQL queries and store the results.

4. Conclusion

In this chapter, we covered:

- **SQL and NoSQL databases**, understanding their differences and use cases.
- How to connect Python to **SQLite**, **MySQL**, and **MongoDB** using appropriate libraries.

- A **real-world example** of building a **contact manager** that stores data in an SQLite database, where we learned how to perform basic CRUD operations (Create, Read, Update, Delete).

Working with databases is crucial for applications that need persistent storage, and understanding how to interact with both SQL and NoSQL databases will help you design efficient, scalable applications. In the next chapter, we will explore **data manipulation** using **Pandas**, a powerful library for handling structured data in Python.

CHAPTER 17

INTRODUCTION TO PYTHON LIBRARIES AND FRAMEWORKS

In this chapter, we will explore the power of **Python libraries** and **frameworks**. These tools allow developers to accomplish complex tasks efficiently without reinventing the wheel. Python's rich ecosystem of libraries and frameworks makes it one of the most versatile programming languages, enabling you to work in fields such as data analysis, web development, machine learning, and more.

We will focus on some essential libraries, including **NumPy**, **pandas**, **requests**, and **Flask**. Additionally, we will walk through a **real-world example** of setting up a simple web server using the **Flask** framework.

1. Overview of Essential Python Libraries

1.1 NumPy

NumPy (Numerical Python) is a powerful library used for numerical computing. It provides support for **arrays**, **matrices**, and a large collection of mathematical functions to operate on these data structures.

- **Key Features**:
    - **ndarray**: The core object of NumPy, which allows you to store and manipulate large datasets efficiently.
    - **Mathematical functions**: NumPy includes many functions for performing operations like addition, multiplication, statistics, and linear algebra.
    - **Broadcasting**: NumPy arrays support broadcasting, a feature that allows operations on arrays of different shapes.

Example:

```python

import numpy as np

# Creating a NumPy array
arr = np.array([1, 2, 3, 4, 5])

# Perform element-wise addition
result = arr + 5
print(result)  # Output: [ 6  7  8  9 10]
```

1.2 pandas

pandas is a fast, powerful, and flexible open-source data analysis and manipulation library. It is built on top of **NumPy** and is ideal for working with structured data, such as **tables** (DataFrames) and **time series**.

- **Key Features**:
    - **DataFrame**: The central data structure in pandas, which is similar to a table or a spreadsheet, with rows and columns.
    - **Data manipulation**: pandas makes it easy to filter, aggregate, merge, and transform data.
    - **Data cleaning**: It provides powerful tools for handling missing data, removing duplicates, and reshaping data.

Example:

```python
python

import pandas as pd

# Creating a DataFrame
data = {'Name': ['Alice', 'Bob', 'Charlie'],
'Age': [24, 27, 22]}
df = pd.DataFrame(data)
```

```
# Display the DataFrame
print(df)
```

1.3 requests

The **requests** library is an essential tool for working with HTTP requests. It allows you to send HTTP requests to web servers and receive responses, making it easy to interact with REST APIs and web services.

- **Key Features**:
    - **GET, POST, PUT, DELETE**: Requests supports all major HTTP methods for interacting with web services.
    - **Simple syntax**: It abstracts the complexities of handling HTTP requests and responses, making it easy to use.
    - **Handling JSON**: requests makes it simple to work with JSON data, which is commonly used in web APIs.

Example:

```python
import requests
```

```
# Send a GET request
response                                    =
requests.get("https://jsonplaceholder.typicode.
com/posts")

# Check the status code
if response.status_code == 200:
    print(response.json())    # Prints the JSON
response
```

1.4 Flask

Flask is a lightweight web framework for Python. It is widely used for building small-to-medium-sized web applications and APIs. Flask is designed to be simple and flexible, allowing developers to add only the features they need.

- **Key Features**:
    - **Routing**: Flask allows you to map URLs to Python functions (view functions) to define the structure of your web application.
    - **Jinja2 templating**: Flask integrates the Jinja2 templating engine for rendering dynamic HTML.
    - **Extension support**: Flask has a number of extensions to add features like database integration, user authentication, and more.

193

Example:

```python
python

from flask import Flask

# Initialize the Flask application
app = Flask(__name__)

# Define a route and view function
@app.route('/')
def hello_world():
    return 'Hello, World!'

# Run the app
if __name__ == '__main__':
    app.run(debug=True)
```

---

2. When and Why to Use Libraries

2.1 Why Use Libraries?

Libraries provide pre-written code that handles common tasks. They allow you to focus on writing your own application logic rather than dealing with complex underlying systems. Here's why you should use libraries:

- **Efficiency**: Libraries save time by providing well-tested solutions to common problems.

- **Consistency**: Libraries follow established standards and practices, reducing the risk of errors.

- **Maintainability**: Libraries are often maintained and updated by experts, so you benefit from bug fixes and improvements.

- **Community Support**: Popular libraries have large communities of users who contribute to documentation, tutorials, and problem-solving.

2.2 When to Use Libraries

You should use libraries when:

- You need to perform common tasks like data analysis (pandas, NumPy), web development (Flask, Django), or HTTP requests (requests).

- You want to avoid reinventing the wheel and need a proven, optimized solution.

- You need to speed up development by leveraging existing tools.

For example:

- **NumPy** is the go-to library for numerical computations.

- **pandas** is essential when working with tabular data, such as spreadsheets or database tables.

- **requests** is the best choice for interacting with REST APIs or scraping data from websites.

- **Flask** is ideal for building lightweight web applications and APIs quickly.

3. Real-World Example: Setting Up a Simple Web Server Using Flask

Let's now build a **real-world example** where we set up a **simple web server** using the **Flask** framework. This server will handle HTTP requests, display a welcome message, and allow users to submit data through a form.

3.1 Installing Flask

To use Flask, you need to install it. Run the following command:

```bash
```

```bash
pip install flask
```

3.2 Creating a Simple Web Server

Here's a basic example of setting up a web server that displays a welcome message and has a form to submit your name:

```python
from flask import Flask, render_template, request

app = Flask(__name__)

# Home route
@app.route('/')
def home():
    return 'Welcome to the Flask Web Server!'

# Route to handle form submission
@app.route('/greet', methods=['GET', 'POST'])
def greet():
    if request.method == 'POST':
        name = request.form['name']
        return f'Hello, {name}!'
    return render_template('greet_form.html')

# Run the app
if __name__ == '__main__':
    app.run(debug=True)
```

3.3 Creating the HTML Form

Flask uses **Jinja2 templating** to render dynamic HTML. Let's create a simple HTML form (greet_form.html) to submit a name.

html

```
<!DOCTYPE html>
<html lang="en">
<head>
    <meta charset="UTF-8">
    <meta name="viewport" content="width=device-
width, initial-scale=1.0">
    <title>Greet Form</title>
</head>
<body>
    <h1>Enter your name</h1>
    <form action="/greet" method="POST">
        <input       type="text"      name="name"
placeholder="Your Name" required>
        <button type="submit">Submit</button>
    </form>
</body>
</html>
```

3.4 How It Works

1. The **home route** (/) returns a simple welcome message.

2. The **/greet route** handles both GET and POST requests. If the user submits the form (via POST), the server displays a personalized greeting using the name entered in the form.

3. The **HTML form** sends a POST request to /greet when the user submits their name.

Running the Flask App

To run the Flask app, save the Python script and HTML file, and run the Python script:

```bash
bash
```

```bash
python app.py
```

Visit http://127.0.0.1:5000/ in your web browser to see the app in action.

---

4. Conclusion

In this chapter, we:

- Explored some essential Python libraries, including **NumPy**, **pandas**, **requests**, and **Flask**, which are widely used in various fields like data science, web development, and API interactions.

- Discussed **when and why to use libraries**, emphasizing how they save time and effort by providing pre-built, optimized solutions.

- Built a **real-world example** by setting up a simple web server using **Flask**, showcasing how to handle HTTP requests and interact with HTML forms.

Libraries and frameworks are powerful tools that make Python development faster and more efficient. In the next chapter, we will dive into **Python testing** and explore techniques for writing automated tests to ensure the reliability of your applications.

CHAPTER 18

DECORATORS AND HIGHER-ORDER FUNCTIONS

In this chapter, we will explore two advanced Python concepts: **decorators** and **higher-order functions**. These features allow us to write more flexible, reusable, and concise code. We will first understand how **decorators** modify the behavior of functions, and then we'll dive into **higher-order functions** like `map()`, `filter()`, and `reduce()`, which allow for more functional programming techniques in Python.

To make these concepts clearer, we will work through a **real-world example** of using decorators to log function calls.

1. Understanding Decorators and How They Modify Functions

1.1 What is a Decorator?

A **decorator** in Python is a special type of function that allows you to modify or extend the behavior of other functions or methods without modifying their actual code. In simple terms, a decorator "wraps" a function, adding functionality before or after the original function runs.

Decorators are commonly used for:

- **Logging** function calls.
- **Measuring** execution time.
- **Authorization** and authentication in web frameworks.

1.2 How Do Decorators Work?

A decorator is a function that takes another function as its argument and returns a new function that enhances the original function's behavior. Decorators are applied to a function using the @ syntax.

Example:

python

```
def simple_decorator(func):
    def wrapper():
        print("Before the function is called.")
        func()
        print("After the function is called.")
    return wrapper
```

```
@simple_decorator
def greet():
    print("Hello, world!")

greet()  # Output will show both the original and
added behavior.
```

In this example:

- simple_decorator is a decorator that takes the function greet() as an argument.
- It returns a new function wrapper() that adds behavior before and after calling the original greet() function.
- The @simple_decorator syntax is shorthand for greet = simple_decorator(greet).

1.3 Decorator Syntax

Using decorators is simple, thanks to Python's **@decorator** syntax. This is a more concise way of applying decorators to functions.

Example:

```python

def my_decorator(func):
```

```
def wrapper():
    print("Before the function")
    func()
    print("After the function")
return wrapper

@my_decorator
def say_hello():
    print("Hello!")

say_hello()
```

Output:

```
pgsql


Before the function
Hello!
After the function
```

In this example, `my_decorator` wraps the `say_hello` function, adding extra behavior before and after it runs.

---

2. Higher-Order Functions: `map()`, `filter()`, and `reduce()`

2.1 What are Higher-Order Functions?

A **higher-order function** is a function that either:

- Takes one or more functions as arguments.
- Returns a function as its result.

In Python, functions like `map()`, `filter()`, and `reduce()` are examples of higher-order functions. They allow for more concise and expressive code when working with sequences like lists.

2.2 `map()` Function

The `map()` function applies a given function to all items in an input list (or iterable) and returns an iterator with the results.

Syntax:

```python

map(function, iterable)
```

Example: Using `map()` to square each number in a list.

```python

numbers = [1, 2, 3, 4, 5]

# Define a function to square numbers
def square(n):
```

205

```
    return n ** 2

# Use map to apply square to each number
squared_numbers = map(square, numbers)

# Convert the map object to a list and print it
print(list(squared_numbers))  # Output: [1, 4, 9,
16, 25]
```

Here, `map()` applies the `square()` function to each element in the `numbers` list.

2.3 `filter()` Function

The `filter()` function filters the elements of an iterable based on a function that returns a boolean value (`True` or `False`). It returns an iterator with only those elements that evaluate to `True`.

Syntax:

```
python
```

```
filter(function, iterable)
```

Example: Using `filter()` to find even numbers in a list.

```
python
```

```
numbers = [1, 2, 3, 4, 5, 6]


# Define a function to check if a number is even
def is_even(n):
    return n % 2 == 0


# Use filter to get only even numbers
even_numbers = filter(is_even, numbers)


# Convert the filter object to a list and print
it
print(list(even_numbers))   # Output: [2, 4, 6]
```

In this example, filter() returns a list of only the numbers that are even.

2.4 reduce() Function

The reduce() function is used to apply a function cumulatively to the items in an iterable. It combines the elements in the iterable into a single result. The reduce() function is part of the functools module, so you must import it.

Syntax:

```
python
```

```
from functools import reduce
reduce(function, iterable)
```

Example: Using reduce() to compute the sum of a list.

```python
from functools import reduce

numbers = [1, 2, 3, 4, 5]

# Define a function to sum two numbers
def add(x, y):
    return x + y

# Use reduce to apply the add function
cumulatively
total = reduce(add, numbers)

print(total)   # Output: 15
```

Here, reduce() applies the add() function to the elements of the numbers list, cumulatively adding them together.

---

3. Real-World Example: Logging Function Calls Using Decorators

Now let's create a real-world example where we use **decorators** to **log function calls**. This is a common use case for decorators, especially when you want to track function execution in a program.

3.1 Creating a Logging Decorator

We will create a decorator that logs the name of the function being called and the arguments it was called with.

python

```
def log_function_call(func):
    def wrapper(*args, **kwargs):
        print(f"Calling {func.__name__} with arguments: {args} and keyword arguments: {kwargs}")
        result = func(*args, **kwargs)
        print(f"{func.__name__} returned: {result}")
        return result
    return wrapper
```

In this example:

- The `log_function_call` decorator logs the function name, its arguments, and the return value each time the decorated function is called.

- `*args` and `**kwargs` allow the decorator to accept any number of positional and keyword arguments.

3.2 Applying the Decorator

Let's apply this decorator to a couple of simple functions.

python

```python
@log_function_call
def add(a, b):
    return a + b

@log_function_call
def greet(name="World"):
    return f"Hello, {name}!"

# Calling the functions
add(3, 5)
greet(name="Alice")
```

Output:

yaml

```
Calling add with arguments: (3, 5) and keyword
arguments: {}
add returned: 8
```

```
Calling greet with arguments: () and keyword
arguments: {'name': 'Alice'}
greet returned: Hello, Alice!
```

In this example:

- The add() function and greet() function are wrapped by the log_function_call decorator, which logs the function call details.
- The decorator prints out the arguments passed, the function's return value, and the function name each time a decorated function is called.

---

4. Conclusion

In this chapter, we learned:

- **Decorators**: Functions that modify the behavior of other functions by "wrapping" them with additional functionality. We used a decorator to log function calls and results.
- **Higher-Order Functions**: Functions like map(), filter(), and reduce() that accept other functions as arguments and return new functions or iterables. These functions help to write cleaner, more concise code.

- A **real-world example** of using decorators to log function calls, which is a common use case in logging, monitoring, and debugging.

Decorators and higher-order functions are powerful features of Python that enable more functional programming styles and help to write cleaner, more maintainable code. In the next chapter, we will explore **Python testing techniques** and best practices for writing automated tests to ensure the reliability of your code.

CHAPTER 19

MULTITHREADING AND MULTIPROCESSING

In this chapter, we will dive into two powerful techniques in Python for handling concurrent execution: **multithreading** and **multiprocessing**. These concepts are essential for improving the performance of programs that need to perform multiple tasks at once, especially when working with I/O-bound or CPU-bound operations.

We will discuss the differences between **threading** and **multiprocessing**, explore when to use each approach, and then implement a **real-world example** where we parallelize web scraping tasks to demonstrate how multithreading and multiprocessing can be leveraged to speed up applications.

1. The Difference Between Threading and Multiprocessing

1.1 Threading

Threading allows you to run multiple tasks concurrently within a single process. Each thread runs in the same memory space, sharing resources such as memory, file handles, and variables. This makes threading an excellent choice for I/O-bound tasks, where the program spends a lot of time waiting for external resources (e.g., reading files, making network requests).

- **Threading Characteristics**:
    - **Lightweight**: Threads share the same memory space, which makes them faster to create and manage than processes.
    - **I/O-bound tasks**: Threading works best when your program is waiting for external operations (e.g., web scraping, file I/O, database queries).
    - **Global Interpreter Lock (GIL)**: In CPython (the default Python implementation), the GIL prevents multiple threads from executing Python bytecodes simultaneously in a single process. This means threading may not provide performance improvements for CPU-bound tasks.

Example: Threading can be useful for making multiple web requests concurrently without blocking the main program.

214

1.2 Multiprocessing

Multiprocessing, on the other hand, involves creating multiple processes, each with its own independent memory space. This allows you to take full advantage of multi-core processors, making it ideal for **CPU-bound tasks** that require significant computation.

- **Multiprocessing Characteristics**:
    - **Independent memory space**: Each process runs in its own memory space, avoiding the issues caused by the GIL.
    - **CPU-bound tasks**: Multiprocessing is ideal for tasks that involve heavy computation (e.g., image processing, data analysis).
    - **Overhead**: Processes are heavier than threads because they each have their own memory space, which results in more overhead when creating and managing them.

Example: Multiprocessing is better suited for tasks like processing large datasets in parallel, where each task runs independently and benefits from running on separate CPU cores.

1.3 Key Differences Between Threading and Multiprocessing:

Feature	Threading	Multiprocessing
Memory	Shared memory space among threads.	Each process has its own memory space.
Concurrency	Ideal for I/O-bound tasks (e.g., web scraping).	Ideal for CPU-bound tasks (e.g., calculations).
Performance	Limited by the GIL for CPU-bound tasks.	Utilizes multiple CPU cores for parallelism.
Overhead	Lower overhead, as threads share resources.	Higher overhead due to process isolation.
Complexity	Easier to manage for simpler concurrent tasks.	More complex due to process communication.

2. When to Use Each Approach

- **Use threading**:
    - ○ When your program is **I/O-bound**, such as when performing multiple I/O operations like web

scraping, downloading files, or querying a database.

- o When you need lightweight concurrent tasks that share data and resources efficiently.

- **Use multiprocessing**:

- o When your program is **CPU-bound**, such as performing heavy computations like image processing, scientific simulations, or machine learning.

- o When you need to make use of multiple CPU cores to achieve better performance.

In general:

- **I/O-bound tasks**: Use threading for better performance.
- **CPU-bound tasks**: Use multiprocessing to fully utilize multi-core CPUs.

---

3. Real-World Example: Parallelizing Web Scraping Tasks

In this real-world example, we'll demonstrate how to speed up a **web scraping** task by using **threading** and **multiprocessing**.

Scenario:

- We need to scrape data from multiple websites. Without concurrency, scraping these websites sequentially could take a long time, especially if we're scraping many pages.
- We will compare the performance of **threading** and **multiprocessing** by scraping multiple pages concurrently.

3.1 Setting Up the Web Scraping Task

We will scrape data from a website using the `requests` library to fetch the content and `BeautifulSoup` from `bs4` to parse the HTML.

Install Required Libraries:

bash

```
pip install requests beautifulsoup4
```

3.2 Web Scraping Using Threading

Let's start by using **threading** to scrape multiple web pages concurrently. We'll use the `ThreadPoolExecutor` from the `concurrent.futures` module to manage multiple threads.

Example: Web Scraping with Threading

```python
python

import requests
from bs4 import BeautifulSoup
from concurrent.futures import ThreadPoolExecutor
import time

# Function to scrape a single page
def scrape_page(url):
    print(f"Scraping {url}")
    response = requests.get(url)
    soup = BeautifulSoup(response.text, 'html.parser')
    return soup.title.string

# List of URLs to scrape
urls = [
    "https://example.com/page1",
    "https://example.com/page2",
    "https://example.com/page3",
    # Add more URLs as needed
]

# Use ThreadPoolExecutor to scrape pages concurrently
start_time = time.time()
with ThreadPoolExecutor() as executor:
```

```
    results  =  list(executor.map(scrape_page,
urls))
```

```
print(f"Scraped    {len(urls)}    pages    in
{time.time() - start_time} seconds.")
```

In this example:

- We use `ThreadPoolExecutor` to manage multiple threads that call the `scrape_page()` function concurrently.
- Each thread sends a GET request to scrape a webpage and extract the page title using BeautifulSoup.

3.3 Web Scraping Using Multiprocessing

Next, let's use **multiprocessing** to parallelize the web scraping task. Since web scraping is an I/O-bound task, threading is often sufficient, but for comparison, we'll implement multiprocessing as well.

Example: Web Scraping with Multiprocessing

```python

from multiprocessing import Pool
```

```python
# Function to scrape a single page
def scrape_page(url):
    print(f"Scraping {url}")
    response = requests.get(url)
    soup      =      BeautifulSoup(response.text,
'html.parser')
    return soup.title.string

# List of URLs to scrape
urls = [
    "https://example.com/page1",
    "https://example.com/page2",
    "https://example.com/page3",
    # Add more URLs as needed
]

# Use Pool to scrape pages concurrently using
multiple processes
start_time = time.time()
with Pool() as pool:
    results = pool.map(scrape_page, urls)

print(f"Scraped      {len(urls)}      pages      in
{time.time() - start_time} seconds.")
```

In this example:

- We use the `Pool` class from the `multiprocessing` module to parallelize the `scrape_page()` function across multiple processes.
- Each process fetches a webpage and extracts the title, running in parallel to the other processes.

3.4 Comparing Performance

By comparing the execution times of both approaches, we can determine which method performs better for this particular web scraping task. Since web scraping is typically I/O-bound, **threading** should provide significant performance improvements over a sequential approach, but **multiprocessing** may not provide a substantial speedup because the tasks are I/O-bound and not CPU-bound.

---

4. Conclusion

In this chapter, we learned:

- The differences between **threading** and **multiprocessing**, and when to use each approach based on whether your tasks are I/O-bound or CPU-bound.
- How to use **threading** and **multiprocessing** for concurrent execution in Python.

- A **real-world example** where we parallelized web scraping tasks using both threading and multiprocessing to speed up the process.

In practice:

- For **I/O-bound tasks** like web scraping, **threading** is typically sufficient and more lightweight.
- For **CPU-bound tasks** that require heavy computation, **multiprocessing** is the better option, as it can take full advantage of multi-core processors.

In the next chapter, we will dive into **Python testing** techniques and best practices for writing automated tests to ensure the reliability and correctness of your code.

CHAPTER 20

INTRODUCTION TO REGULAR EXPRESSIONS

In this chapter, we will explore **regular expressions** (regex) and how to use them in Python for **pattern matching**. Regular expressions provide a powerful way to search, match, and manipulate text based on specific patterns. We will also look at a **real-world example** where we use regular expressions to parse log files, which is a common use case for regex.

1. Using Regular Expressions for Pattern Matching in Python

1.1 What are Regular Expressions?

A **regular expression** (or regex) is a sequence of characters that defines a search pattern. It is often used for:

- **Searching**: Finding specific text in a string.
- **Matching**: Checking if a string conforms to a specific pattern.

- **Replacing**: Substituting text that matches a pattern with other text.
- **Splitting**: Dividing text based on a pattern.

Regular expressions are widely used in text processing tasks like form validation, data extraction, and log parsing.

1.2 Python's re Module

Python has a built-in module called **re** that provides support for working with regular expressions. This module includes functions like `search()`, `match()`, `findall()`, `sub()`, and `split()` to perform various operations using regular expressions.

Common re Functions:

- **`re.match(pattern, string)`**: Checks if the pattern matches the beginning of the string.
- **`re.search(pattern, string)`**: Searches the string for the first occurrence of the pattern.
- **`re.findall(pattern, string)`**: Returns all non-overlapping matches of the pattern in the string as a list.
- **`re.sub(pattern, replacement, string)`**: Replaces occurrences of the pattern in the string with the specified replacement.

- `re.split(pattern, string)`: Splits the string into a list based on the specified pattern.

1.3 Basic Regular Expression Syntax

Here are some fundamental regex components:

- `.`: Matches any character except a newline.
- `^`: Anchors the pattern to the beginning of the string.
- `$`: Anchors the pattern to the end of the string.
- `[]`: Matches any one character inside the square brackets (e.g., `[a-z]` matches any lowercase letter).
- `*`: Matches zero or more occurrences of the preceding character.
- `+`: Matches one or more occurrences of the preceding character.
- `{n,m}`: Matches between n and m occurrences of the preceding character.
- `\d`: Matches any digit (equivalent to `[0-9]`).
- `\w`: Matches any word character (letters, digits, and underscores).
- `\s`: Matches any whitespace character (spaces, tabs, newlines).

1.4 Using Regular Expressions in Python

Let's now look at how we can use the `re` module to perform pattern matching with regular expressions.

Example: Simple Regular Expression Matching

```python
python

import re

# Sample string
text = "The quick brown fox jumps over the lazy
dog"

# Regular expression pattern to match the word
'fox'
pattern = r"fox"

# Use re.search() to search for the pattern
match = re.search(pattern, text)

if match:
    print(f"Match found: {match.group()}")
else:
    print("No match found.")
```

Output:

```sql
sql
```

227

```
Match found: fox
```

In this example:

- We use `re.search()` to search for the word `fox` in the text.
- If the pattern is found, `match.group()` returns the matched string.

1.5 Special Characters and Character Classes

Regular expressions allow you to match specific kinds of characters with special syntax.

- **\d**: Matches any digit (0-9).
- **\w**: Matches any alphanumeric character (a-z, A-Z, 0-9).
- **\s**: Matches any whitespace character (spaces, tabs, etc.).
- **[a-z]**: Matches any lowercase letter.
- **[^a-z]**: Matches any character that is not a lowercase letter.

2. Real-World Example: Parsing Logs with Regular Expressions

Let's now apply regular expressions to a **real-world example**: parsing log files. Logs often contain structured data with timestamps, log levels (e.g., INFO, ERROR), and messages. We will use regular expressions to extract relevant information from log entries.

2.1 Sample Log File

Consider the following sample log file (`app.log`):

```pgsql

2022-09-01 12:30:45 INFO User logged in
2022-09-01 12:35:10 ERROR Failed to connect to database
2022-09-01 12:40:05 WARNING Low disk space
2022-09-01 12:45:30 INFO User logged out
```

We want to:

1. Extract the **timestamp**.
2. Extract the **log level** (e.g., INFO, ERROR, WARNING).
3. Extract the **message**.

2.2 Using Regular Expressions to Parse the Log File

We will use a regular expression to match each log entry and extract the relevant fields: timestamp, log level, and message.

python

```
import re

# Sample log entries
logs = """
2022-09-01 12:30:45 INFO User logged in
2022-09-01 12:35:10 ERROR Failed to connect to
database
2022-09-01 12:40:05 WARNING Low disk space
2022-09-01 12:45:30 INFO User logged out
"""

# Regular expression to match log entries
pattern          =          r"(\d{4}-\d{2}-\d{2}
\d{2}:\d{2}:\d{2})\s(\w+)\s(.+)"

# Use re.findall() to extract all matches
matches = re.findall(pattern, logs)

# Print the matches
for match in matches:
    timestamp, log_level, message = match
```

```
print(f"Timestamp: {timestamp}, Log Level:
{log_level}, Message: {message}")
```

Output:

pgsql

Timestamp: 2022-09-01 12:30:45, Log Level: INFO,
Message: User logged in
Timestamp: 2022-09-01 12:35:10, Log Level: ERROR,
Message: Failed to connect to database
Timestamp: 2022-09-01 12:40:05, Log Level:
WARNING, Message: Low disk space
Timestamp: 2022-09-01 12:45:30, Log Level: INFO,
Message: User logged out

Explanation:

- The regular expression (\d{4}-\d{2}-\d{2}
  \d{2}:\d{2}:\d{2})\s(\w+)\s(.+) consists of
  three groups:
  - (\d{4}-\d{2}-\d{2}
    \d{2}:\d{2}:\d{2}): Matches the timestamp
    (e.g., 2022-09-01 12:30:45).
  - (\w+): Matches the log level (e.g., INFO,
    ERROR).
  - (.+): Matches the message part of the log entry
    (e.g., User logged in).

231

- `re.findall()` returns a list of tuples, each containing the matched timestamp, log level, and message.

2.3 Handling More Complex Log Patterns

If the log entries become more complex, with more varied log formats, you can adjust the regular expression to capture different patterns or optional fields. Regular expressions allow for great flexibility in defining what to match.

---

3. Conclusion

In this chapter, we:

- Learned how to use **regular expressions** in Python for powerful **pattern matching** with the `re` module.
- Explored basic regular expression syntax, including how to match specific characters and groups.
- Applied regular expressions to a **real-world log parsing example**, where we extracted timestamps, log levels, and messages from a sample log file.

Regular expressions are a crucial tool for text processing, especially when dealing with structured text such as logs, configuration files, and data extraction. Mastering regex will greatly enhance your ability to solve complex text manipulation problems in Python.

In the next chapter, we will dive into **Python testing** techniques, including how to write automated tests to ensure your code is correct and reliable.

CHAPTER 21

WEB DEVELOPMENT WITH FLASK

In this chapter, we will explore **web development** with the **Flask** framework, one of Python's most popular lightweight web frameworks. Flask is known for its simplicity and flexibility, making it a great choice for both beginners and experienced developers. We will walk through the process of building a simple web application — a **To-Do List app** — and integrate the frontend with HTML, CSS, and JavaScript to create an interactive user interface.

1. Introduction to Web Development with Flask

1.1 What is Flask?

Flask is a lightweight web framework for building web applications in Python. Unlike more complex frameworks like Django, Flask provides the essential tools to get a web app running, but it gives you the flexibility to add additional features as needed. Flask is perfect for small-to-medium-sized applications and APIs.

Key Features of Flask:

- **Minimalistic**: Flask does not come with built-in features like a database or form handling system, giving you the freedom to choose the tools you need.
- **Extensible**: Flask supports a wide range of extensions for adding features such as form validation, authentication, and database integration.
- **Jinja2 Templating**: Flask uses **Jinja2**, a powerful templating engine that allows you to generate dynamic HTML.
- **Built-in Development Server**: Flask comes with a built-in server for testing and development.

1.2 Installing Flask

To get started with Flask, you need to install it. You can install Flask using `pip`:

bash

```
pip install flask
```

1.3 Flask Application Structure

A typical Flask application has a simple structure, like this:

php

```
my_flask_app/
|
├── app.py              # The main application file
├── templates/             # HTML files (Jinja2 templates)
|   └── index.html   # Example HTML template
└── static/                # Static files (CSS, JS, images)
        ├── style.css   # Example CSS file
        └── script.js   # Example JavaScript file
```

- **app.py**: Contains the Flask application and routing logic.
- **templates/**: Contains HTML files that are rendered dynamically with Flask's **Jinja2** templating engine.
- **static/**: Stores static files such as CSS, JavaScript, and images.

---

2. Building a Simple Web Application: To-Do List App

Let's now build a simple **To-Do List app**. This app will allow users to add tasks, mark them as completed, and delete tasks. We will use **Flask** for the backend, and HTML, CSS, and JavaScript for the frontend.

2.1 Setting Up the Flask Application

Start by creating the app.py file, which will define the routes and handle the logic of the To-Do List app.

python

```python
from flask import Flask, render_template,
request, redirect, url_for

app = Flask(__name__)

# In-memory list to store tasks (this will be
cleared when the app restarts)
tasks = []

# Home route that displays the to-do list
@app.route('/')
def home():
    return          render_template('index.html',
tasks=tasks)

# Route to add a new task
@app.route('/add', methods=['POST'])
```

```python
def add_task():
    task = request.form.get('task')
    if task:
        tasks.append({'task': task, 'completed':
False})
    return redirect(url_for('home'))


# Route to mark a task as completed
@app.route('/complete/<int:task_id>')
def complete_task(task_id):
    tasks[task_id]['completed'] = True
    return redirect(url_for('home'))


# Route to delete a task
@app.route('/delete/<int:task_id>')
def delete_task(task_id):
    tasks.pop(task_id)
    return redirect(url_for('home'))


if __name__ == '__main__':
    app.run(debug=True)
```

Explanation:

- The **home route** (/) renders the list of tasks from the tasks list.
- The **add_task route** (/add) adds a new task to the tasks list when the user submits a form.

- The **complete_task route** (`/complete/<task_id>`) marks a task as completed by setting its `completed` status to `True`.
- The **delete_task route** (`/delete/<task_id>`) removes a task from the list.

2.2 Creating the Frontend: HTML, CSS, and JavaScript

Next, we need to create the frontend of the application using **HTML** for structure, **CSS** for styling, and **JavaScript** for interactivity.

2.3 HTML Template (index.html)

Create the `templates/index.html` file to display the tasks and the form to add new tasks.

html

```html
<!DOCTYPE html>
<html lang="en">
<head>
    <meta charset="UTF-8">
    <meta name="viewport" content="width=device-width, initial-scale=1.0">
```

```html
<title>To-Do List</title>
<link       rel="stylesheet"       href="{{
url_for('static', filename='style.css') }}">
</head>
<body>
    <div class="container">
        <h1>To-Do List</h1>


        <!-- Form to add a new task -->
        <form action="/add" method="POST">
            <input    type="text"    name="task"
placeholder="Enter a new task" required>
            <button          type="submit">Add
Task</button>
        </form>


        <ul>
            <!-- Loop through tasks and display
them -->
            {% for task in tasks %}
            <li    class="{{    'completed'    if
task.completed else '' }}">
                {{ task.task }}
                <!-- Mark task as completed -->
                {% if not task.completed %}
                <a           href="/complete/{{
loop.index0 }}">Mark as Completed</a>
                {% endif %}
                <!-- Delete task -->
```

```
        <a href="/delete/{{ loop.index0
}}">Delete</a>
        </li>
        {% endfor %}
      </ul>
    </div>

    <script      src="{{      url_for('static',
filename='script.js') }}"></script>
</body>
</html>
```

Explanation:

- The   {{   url_for('static',
  filename='style.css') }} syntax is used to link to
  static files like CSS and JavaScript.

- The {{ 'completed' if task.completed else
  '' }} syntax is used to apply a CSS class to completed
  tasks.

- We loop through the tasks list and display each task
  along with the options to mark it as completed or delete
  it.

2.4 Styling with CSS (style.css)

241

Create a `static/style.css` file to add some basic styles to the app.

css

```css
body {
    font-family: Arial, sans-serif;
    background-color: #f4f4f9;
    padding: 20px;
}


.container {
    max-width: 600px;
    margin: 0 auto;
    background-color: white;
    padding: 20px;
    border-radius: 8px;
    box-shadow: 0 0 10px rgba(0, 0, 0, 0.1);
}


h1 {
    text-align: center;
}


form {
    display: flex;
    justify-content: space-between;
}
```

```
input {
    width: 80%;
    padding: 10px;
    margin-right: 10px;
    border: 1px solid #ccc;
    border-radius: 4px;
}

button {
    padding: 10px 20px;
    background-color: #28a745;
    color: white;
    border: none;
    border-radius: 4px;
    cursor: pointer;
}

button:hover {
    background-color: #218838;
}

ul {
    list-style-type: none;
    padding: 0;
}

li {
    display: flex;
    justify-content: space-between;
```

```css
    padding: 10px;
    margin: 5px 0;
    background-color: #f9f9f9;
    border-radius: 4px;
}

li.completed {
    text-decoration: line-through;
    background-color: #e9ecef;
}

a {
    color: #007bff;
    text-decoration: none;
}

a:hover {
    text-decoration: underline;
}
```

Explanation:

- The styles make the app look clean and organized, with a responsive layout.
- The completed tasks have a line-through style applied and a different background color.

2.5 Adding Interactivity with JavaScript (script.js)

Although our app doesn't require heavy JavaScript, we can add some basic interactivity, like dynamically handling task completion without a page refresh.

```javascript
document.addEventListener("DOMContentLoaded",
function() {
    const             taskLinks             =
document.querySelectorAll("a[href^='/complete']
");

    taskLinks.forEach(link => {
        link.addEventListener("click",
function(e) {
            e.preventDefault();
            const             taskId             =
this.getAttribute("href").split("/").pop();

this.parentElement.classList.add("completed");
            this.textContent = "Completed";
        });
    });
});
```

Explanation:

- This script adds an event listener to each "Mark as Completed" link. When clicked, it marks the task as completed by adding a CSS class and changing the text content.

---

3. Conclusion

In this chapter, we:

- Learned the basics of **Flask** and how to set up a simple web application.
- Built a **To-Do List app** that allows users to add tasks, mark them as completed, and delete them.
- Integrated the **frontend** with **HTML**, **CSS**, and **JavaScript** to create an interactive and visually appealing user interface.

Flask provides a simple and flexible foundation for web development. This hands-on example shows how Flask can be used to build dynamic applications, while HTML, CSS, and JavaScript provide the structure, style, and interactivity needed for a complete web application.

In the next chapter, we will look at **database integration** in Flask, showing how to store user data in a database and enhance the functionality of our To-Do List app.

CHAPTER 22

BUILDING A COMMAND-LINE APPLICATION

In this chapter, we will learn how to build a **command-line application** in Python using the `argparse` module. Command-line applications are a powerful way to automate tasks and interact with systems. We will explore how to handle **command-line arguments** using `argparse`, and then create a **real-world example**: a **file organizer tool** that organizes files into directories based on their file types (e.g., images, documents, etc.).

1. Using `argparse` for Handling Command-Line Arguments

1.1 What is `argparse`?

The **argparse** module is part of the Python standard library and provides an easy way to handle command-line arguments in Python programs. It allows you to define what arguments the program requires, parse them, and handle them accordingly.

Key Features of `argparse`:

- **Command-line argument parsing**: It allows you to specify what command-line arguments the program accepts and automatically generates help messages.
- **Optional and positional arguments**: It supports both required (positional) and optional arguments.
- **Argument types**: You can specify argument types (e.g., strings, integers) and default values.

1.2 Basic `argparse` Usage

Here's an example of using `argparse` to handle simple command-line arguments.

```python
python

import argparse

# Initialize the parser
parser = argparse.ArgumentParser(description="Simple argument parsing example.")

# Add arguments
parser.add_argument('name', type=str, help="Your name")
parser.add_argument('age', type=int, help="Your age")
```

```
# Parse the arguments
args = parser.parse_args()

# Use the arguments
print(f"Hello {args.name}, you are {args.age}
years old.")
```

Running the script:

```
bash
```

```
python script.py John 25
```

Output:

```
sql
```

```
Hello John, you are 25 years old.
```

In this example:

- We used `parser.add_argument()` to define two arguments: name (a required string) and age (a required integer).
- We used `args.name` and `args.age` to access the values provided by the user.

1.3 Optional Arguments

You can also specify **optional arguments**, which are not required to run the program. These are typically preceded by a -- or - when invoked.

```python
python
```

```python
import argparse

# Initialize the parser
parser                                    =
argparse.ArgumentParser(description="Optional
argument example.")

# Add an optional argument
parser.add_argument('--greeting',        type=str,
default="Hello", help="A greeting message")

# Parse the arguments
args = parser.parse_args()

# Use the argument
print(f"{args.greeting}, World!")
```

Running the script:

```bash
bash
```

```bash
python script.py --greeting "Hi"
```

Output:

```
Hi, World!
```

In this example, --greeting is an optional argument with a default value of "Hello" if not provided.

1.4 Argument Types and Default Values

argparse also allows you to specify argument types and provide default values when arguments are not provided.

```python
python

import argparse

# Initialize the parser
parser                                          =
argparse.ArgumentParser(description="Argument
types and default values.")

# Add an argument with a default value
parser.add_argument('--count',          type=int,
default=10, help="The number of times to repeat
the message")

# Parse the arguments
```

251

```
args = parser.parse_args()

# Use the argument
for _ in range(args.count):
    print("This is a repeated message.")
```

Running the script:

```bash
```

```
python script.py --count 3
```

Output:

```csharp
```

```
This is a repeated message.
This is a repeated message.
This is a repeated message.
```

If you don't provide the `--count` argument, it defaults to 10.

---

2. Real-World Example: Building a File Organizer Tool

Now let's build a **real-world command-line application** that organizes files in a specified directory by their **file type**. For

252

example, it will move `.jpg` files to an "Images" folder, `.pdf` files to a "Documents" folder, and so on.

The steps are:

1. Use `argparse` to accept a directory path as a command-line argument.
2. Identify files based on their extension.
3. Create folders based on file types (if they don't already exist).
4. Move the files into the corresponding folders.

2.1 Setting Up the File Organizer Script

Let's start by creating the script that will take the source directory and organize the files.

```python

import os
import shutil
import argparse

# Define a function to organize files
def organize_files(directory):
    # Define the file categories
    categories = {
```

```
        'Images':    ['.jpg',    '.jpeg',    '.png',
'.gif'],
        'Documents': ['.pdf', '.docx', '.txt',
'.csv'],
        'Videos': ['.mp4', '.mov', '.avi'],
        'Audio': ['.mp3', '.wav', '.flac'],
        'Archives': ['.zip', '.tar', '.gz']
    }


    # Loop through the files in the provided
directory
    for filename in os.listdir(directory):
        file_path    =    os.path.join(directory,
filename)

        if os.path.isfile(file_path):    # Only
consider files (not subdirectories)
            file_ext                          =
os.path.splitext(filename)[1].lower()

            # Find the appropriate category
            for    category,    extensions    in
categories.items():
                if file_ext in extensions:
                    # Create category folder if
it doesn't exist
                    category_folder          =
os.path.join(directory, category)
```

```python
                if                      not
os.path.exists(category_folder):

os.makedirs(category_folder)

                # Move the file to the
appropriate folder
                shutil.move(file_path,
os.path.join(category_folder, filename))
                print(f"Moved: {filename} ->
{category}")
                break

# Initialize the parser
parser                                    =
argparse.ArgumentParser(description="File
Organizer")

# Add a directory argument
parser.add_argument('directory',          type=str,
help="Directory to organize")

# Parse the arguments
args = parser.parse_args()

# Organize the files
organize_files(args.directory)
```

Explanation:

- The `organize_files()` function takes a directory path and organizes files based on their extension.
- We define several categories (e.g., Images, Documents, Videos) and associate file extensions with each category.
- The script uses `os.listdir()` to list all files in the provided directory and `os.path.splitext()` to get the file extension.
- It checks if a folder exists for each category and creates one if necessary using `os.makedirs()`.
- It then moves the files into their corresponding folders using `shutil.move()`.

2.2 Running the File Organizer Tool

To use the file organizer tool, run the script from the command line by providing the path to the directory you want to organize.

Example Command:

```bash
```

```
python file_organizer.py /path/to/your/directory
```

The script will move the files in the specified directory to new subfolders based on their extensions, such as "Images", "Documents", etc.

256

2.3 Enhancing the Tool (Optional)

We can extend this tool by adding features like:

- **Logging**: Record the actions taken (e.g., which files were moved).
- **Recursive directory handling**: Organize files in subdirectories as well.
- **Handling conflicts**: When a file with the same name exists in the destination folder, either overwrite it or append a suffix to the filename.

3. Conclusion

In this chapter, we:

- Learned how to use the `argparse` module to handle command-line arguments in Python.
- Built a **real-world file organizer tool** that organizes files into directories based on their extensions.
- Explored how to add flexibility and customization to a command-line application using `argparse` and Python's built-in file handling functions.

Command-line applications are a great way to automate repetitive tasks and improve productivity. Flask for web applications and `argparse` for command-line tools are just two examples of how Python's versatility allows you to create powerful and useful applications. In the next chapter, we will delve into **automated testing** and how to ensure your applications are functioning as expected.

CHAPTER 23

AUTOMATION WITH PYTHON

In this chapter, we will explore how Python can be used to **automate repetitive tasks**, making your workflow more efficient. We will also learn how to **schedule tasks** using libraries like **schedule** and **APScheduler**, which allow you to automate actions at specified times. To bring everything together, we will build a **real-world example**: an **automated email report generator** that sends reports at scheduled intervals.

1. Writing Scripts to Automate Repetitive Tasks

One of the greatest strengths of Python is its ability to automate tasks that are otherwise time-consuming and repetitive. Whether it's renaming files, sending emails, or scraping websites for data, Python scripts can save time and reduce errors by automating manual processes.

Common Automation Tasks:

- **File Handling**: Automatically renaming, moving, or backing up files.

259

- **Data Processing**: Automating data cleaning, transformation, and analysis.
- **Web Scraping**: Collecting data from websites on a regular basis.
- **Emailing**: Sending routine emails like status reports, reminders, or notifications.
- **System Administration**: Automating system maintenance tasks like backups or monitoring.

1.1 Example: Automating File Renaming

Let's start with a simple example of automating file renaming. Assume you have a folder of images, and you want to rename them by appending the current date to each filename.

```python
import os
import datetime

# Directory containing the files
directory = '/path/to/images'

# Get the current date in YYYY-MM-DD format
today = datetime.date.today()

# Loop through all files in the directory
```

```
for filename in os.listdir(directory):
    if       filename.endswith('.jpg')       or
filename.endswith('.png'):
        new_name = f"{today}_{filename}"
        os.rename(os.path.join(directory,
filename), os.path.join(directory, new_name))
        print(f"Renamed       {filename}       to
{new_name}")
```

Explanation:

- We use `os.listdir()` to list all the files in the specified directory.

- We check if the file is an image (i.e., ends with `.jpg` or `.png`).

- Then, we use `os.rename()` to rename each file by appending the current date to the filename.

1.2 Automating Data Analysis and Report Generation

Python is also powerful for automating data analysis tasks. For instance, you can use libraries like **pandas** to automate data cleaning, processing, and report generation.

```python
python
```

```
import pandas as pd
```

261

```
# Read data from a CSV file
data = pd.read_csv('sales_data.csv')

# Perform some data processing
summary = data.describe()  # Summary statistics

# Generate a report (e.g., save it to a new CSV
file)
summary.to_csv('sales_summary_report.csv')
```

Explanation:

- We read data from a CSV file using **pandas**.
- We use `describe()` to generate summary statistics.
- The result is saved as a new CSV file (`sales_summary_report.csv`), which can be automatically emailed or stored for later use.

---

2. Scheduling Tasks Using `schedule` *or* `APScheduler`

Once you have automated tasks, the next step is to schedule them to run at specific intervals. Python provides several libraries to handle task scheduling.

2.1 Scheduling Tasks with `schedule` Library

The `schedule` library is a simple Python library for scheduling tasks. It allows you to run tasks periodically, such as every minute, hour, or day.

Installing `schedule`:

bash

```bash
pip install schedule
```

Basic Usage:

python

```python
import schedule
import time

# Define a simple task
def task():
    print("Running the scheduled task!")

# Schedule the task to run every 5 seconds
schedule.every(5).seconds.do(task)

# Keep the script running and execute tasks
while True:
    schedule.run_pending()
    time.sleep(1)
```

263

Explanation:

- We define a function `task()` that prints a message.
- Using `schedule.every(5).seconds.do(task)`, we set the task to run every 5 seconds.
- `schedule.run_pending()` is called in a loop to check and run any tasks that are due.

2.2 Scheduling Tasks with `APScheduler`

While `schedule` is simple and effective for many tasks, **APScheduler** (Advanced Python Scheduler) is more powerful and offers more advanced features like job persistence, error handling, and more complex scheduling options.

Installing `APScheduler`:

bash

```
pip install apscheduler
```

Basic Usage:

python

```
from apscheduler.schedulers.blocking import BlockingScheduler
```

```python
import time

# Define a simple task
def task():
    print("Running the scheduled task!")

# Initialize the scheduler
scheduler = BlockingScheduler()

# Schedule the task to run every 10 seconds
scheduler.add_job(task, 'interval', seconds=10)

# Start the scheduler
scheduler.start()
```

Explanation:

- We use `BlockingScheduler` to schedule jobs that will run until the program exits.
- `scheduler.add_job()` schedules the `task()` function to run every 10 seconds.
- `scheduler.start()` keeps the program running and allows the scheduled tasks to execute.

3. Real-World Example: Automating Email Reports

Now let's combine automation and scheduling to create a **real-world example**: an **automated email report generator**. This tool will:

1. Generate a report (e.g., data analysis or system status).
2. Send it via email on a regular schedule.

Steps:

1. Use `schedule` or `APScheduler` to schedule the task.
2. Use the `smtplib` module to send emails via SMTP.
3. Use `pandas` to generate a simple report.

3.1 Sending an Email with Python

Before we automate sending emails, let's set up basic email functionality using Python's built-in `smtplib` library.

```python

import smtplib
from email.mime.text import MIMEText
from email.mime.multipart import MIMEMultipart

def send_email(subject, body, to_email):
    from_email = "your_email@example.com"
    password = "your_password"
```

```
# Set up the MIME
msg = MIMEMultipart()
msg['From'] = from_email
msg['To'] = to_email
msg['Subject'] = subject

msg.attach(MIMEText(body, 'plain'))

# Connect to the SMTP server and send the
email
server = smtplib.SMTP('smtp.example.com',
587)  # Use your SMTP server and port
server.starttls()  # Secure the connection
server.login(from_email, password)
text = msg.as_string()
server.sendmail(from_email, to_email, text)
server.quit()

# Example usage
send_email("Monthly Report", "Here is the report
for this month.", "recipient@example.com")
```

Explanation:

- We use the `smtplib` module to connect to an SMTP server (e.g., Gmail, Outlook).

- The `MIMEMultipart` class allows us to create an email with both a subject and body.

267

- The `sendmail()` method sends the email to the recipient.

3.2 Automating the Report Generation and Email Sending

Now, let's automate the process of sending email reports using **APScheduler**.

python

```python
import pandas as pd
from apscheduler.schedulers.blocking import BlockingScheduler

def generate_report():
    # Generate a simple data report (for example purposes)
    data = {'Name': ['Alice', 'Bob', 'Charlie'], 'Age': [24, 27, 22]}
    df = pd.DataFrame(data)

    # Convert the report to a string (could be saved as CSV, etc.)
    report = df.to_string()

    return report
```

```python
def send_report():
    # Generate the report
    report = generate_report()

    # Send the report via email
    send_email("Monthly Data Report", report,
"recipient@example.com")

# Initialize the scheduler
scheduler = BlockingScheduler()

# Schedule the task to run at 8 AM on the first
day of every month
scheduler.add_job(send_report, 'cron', day=1,
hour=8, minute=0)

# Start the scheduler
scheduler.start()
```

Explanation:

- **generate_report()**: This function creates a simple **pandas DataFrame** with some sample data and converts it to a string (you can modify this to create a more complex report).
- **send_report()**: This function calls generate_report() and then sends the result via email using the previously defined send_email() function.

269

- We use **APScheduler** to schedule the `send_report()` function to run at **8 AM** on the **first day of every month**.

---

4. Conclusion

In this chapter, we:

- Learned how to **automate repetitive tasks** using Python, such as renaming files, processing data, and sending emails.
- Explored how to **schedule tasks** using the `schedule` and `APScheduler` libraries.
- Built a **real-world application** to automate the process of generating and emailing monthly reports, which is a common automation task in many businesses.

Automation with Python is a powerful way to streamline workflows, reduce manual errors, and save time. In the next chapter, we will explore **Python logging** and how to track and record important events in your applications.

CHAPTER 24

DATA SCIENCE WITH PYTHON

In this chapter, we will introduce the basics of **data science** using Python, focusing on three key libraries: **pandas**, **NumPy**, and **Matplotlib**. These libraries are essential for handling and analyzing data, as well as creating visualizations to better understand trends and patterns. We will walk through a **real-world example** of analyzing **sales data** to identify trends and visualize insights.

1. Introduction to Data Science with pandas, NumPy, and Matplotlib

1.1 What is Data Science?

Data Science involves using techniques, algorithms, and systems to extract knowledge and insights from structured and unstructured data. Python has become the language of choice for many data scientists because of its simplicity and the powerful libraries available.

The three libraries we'll focus on are:

271

- **pandas**: A powerful library for data manipulation and analysis. It provides data structures like **DataFrame** for working with structured data.
- **NumPy**: A library for numerical computing in Python. It provides support for arrays and matrices, and allows you to perform mathematical operations on large datasets.
- **Matplotlib**: A library for creating static, animated, and interactive visualizations in Python. It is commonly used to create plots, charts, and other graphical representations of data.

1.2 pandas

pandas is the go-to library for working with **structured data** (e.g., tabular data such as CSVs or Excel files). The primary data structures are:

- **Series**: A one-dimensional array-like object.
- **DataFrame**: A two-dimensional table with rows and columns, similar to a spreadsheet.

1.3 NumPy

NumPy is the fundamental package for numerical computing in Python. It provides support for:

- **Arrays**: NumPy arrays are more efficient than Python lists for handling large datasets.
- **Mathematical functions**: You can perform operations like addition, subtraction, multiplication, and linear algebra with NumPy arrays.

1.4 Matplotlib

Matplotlib is a plotting library for Python. It allows you to create a variety of static, animated, and interactive plots and charts. The most common types of visualizations include:

- **Line plots**
- **Bar charts**
- **Histograms**
- **Scatter plots**

2. Basic Data Analysis Techniques and Visualizations

2.1 Loading and Exploring Data with pandas

The first step in any data analysis task is to load the dataset. We will use **pandas** to read a dataset (e.g., a CSV file) and explore the data.

Example: Loading and Inspecting Data

```python
python

import pandas as pd

# Load the dataset
df = pd.read_csv('sales_data.csv')

# Inspect the first few rows of the data
print(df.head())

# Get summary statistics
print(df.describe())

# Check for missing values
print(df.isnull().sum())
```

Explanation:

- **pd.read_csv()**: Loads the CSV file into a pandas DataFrame.
- **head()**: Displays the first few rows of the DataFrame.
- **describe()**: Generates summary statistics of numeric columns.

- **isnull().sum()**: Checks for any missing values in the dataset.

2.2 Data Cleaning and Preparation

Data cleaning is one of the most important steps in data analysis. This involves handling missing data, correcting data types, and performing any necessary transformations.

Example: Handling Missing Data

python

```
# Fill missing values with the mean of the column
df['Sales']                                    =
df['Sales'].fillna(df['Sales'].mean())

# Drop rows with any missing values
df = df.dropna()
```

Explanation:

- **fillna()**: Fills missing values with a specified value (in this case, the mean of the column).
- **dropna()**: Drops rows that contain any missing values.

2.3 Basic Data Analysis with pandas

Now that the data is cleaned, we can perform some basic analysis.
Let's calculate some summary statistics and find correlations.

Example: Summary Statistics and Correlations

python

```python
# Calculate the total sales
total_sales = df['Sales'].sum()

# Calculate the average sales
average_sales = df['Sales'].mean()

# Calculate the correlation between sales and
advertising budget
correlation                                    =
df['Sales'].corr(df['Advertising'])

print(f"Total Sales: {total_sales}")
print(f"Average Sales: {average_sales}")
print(f"Correlation     between     Sales     and
Advertising: {correlation}")
```

Explanation:

- **sum()**: Calculates the total sales across all rows.
- **mean()**: Calculates the average sales.

276

- **corr()**: Calculates the correlation between two columns (in this case, "Sales" and "Advertising").

---

3. Real-World Example: Analyzing a Dataset of Sales Data and Plotting Trends

---

Let's now put everything together and analyze a **sales dataset**. We will load the data, clean it, perform some basic analysis, and create visualizations to uncover trends.

3.1 Example Dataset: sales_data.csv

Assume the dataset has the following columns:

- **Date**: The date of the sales record.
- **Sales**: The number of sales made on that day.
- **Advertising**: The advertising budget spent on that day.

3.2 Analyzing and Plotting the Data

Now let's load the data, perform some basic analysis, and plot the trends.

```python
```

```python
import pandas as pd
import matplotlib.pyplot as plt

# Load the dataset
df = pd.read_csv('sales_data.csv')

# Handle missing values (optional)
df['Sales']                              =
df['Sales'].fillna(df['Sales'].mean())

# Convert 'Date' to datetime format
df['Date'] = pd.to_datetime(df['Date'])

# Set the Date column as the index
df.set_index('Date', inplace=True)

# Calculate the correlation between sales and
advertising
correlation                              =
df['Sales'].corr(df['Advertising'])

# Print the correlation
print(f"Correlation    between    Sales    and
Advertising: {correlation}")

# Plot Sales vs Advertising
plt.figure(figsize=(10, 6))
plt.scatter(df['Advertising'],    df['Sales'],
color='blue', label='Sales vs Advertising')
```

```
plt.title('Sales vs Advertising')
plt.xlabel('Advertising Budget')
plt.ylabel('Sales')
plt.grid(True)
plt.legend()
plt.show()

# Plot sales trends over time
plt.figure(figsize=(10, 6))
plt.plot(df.index, df['Sales'], color='green',
label='Sales Trend')
plt.title('Sales Trend Over Time')
plt.xlabel('Date')
plt.ylabel('Sales')
plt.grid(True)
plt.legend()
plt.xticks(rotation=45)
plt.show()
```

Explanation:

- **pd.to_datetime()**: Converts the "Date" column to datetime format, which is necessary for time series analysis.
- **set_index('Date')**: Sets the "Date" column as the index, which makes time-based plotting easier.
- **plt.scatter()**: Creates a scatter plot showing the relationship between advertising budget and sales.

279

- `plt.plot()`: Creates a line plot to show the sales trend over time.

- `plt.xticks(rotation=45)`: Rotates the x-axis labels to make them more readable.

3.3 Interpreting the Visualizations

- The **scatter plot** shows the relationship between **advertising** and **sales**. If the points form a pattern, it suggests a correlation between the two variables.

- The **line plot** shows the **sales trend over time**, helping to visualize if there are any seasonal patterns or overall growth in sales.

---

4. Conclusion

In this chapter, we:

- Learned how to use **pandas** for data manipulation, cleaning, and analysis.
- Explored **NumPy** for numerical operations (though we didn't use it in the example, it's commonly used in more complex analyses).
- Used **Matplotlib** to create visualizations like scatter plots and line graphs.

- Applied these concepts to a **real-world example** where we analyzed a sales dataset, calculated correlations, and visualized trends.

Python's powerful data science libraries allow you to manipulate and analyze data with ease, and create informative visualizations that provide valuable insights. In the next chapter, we will dive into **machine learning with Python**, exploring how to use libraries like **scikit-learn** to build predictive models.

CHAPTER 25

SCALING APPLICATIONS WITH DOCKER

In this chapter, we will explore how to **scale applications** using **Docker**, a powerful tool for containerization. We'll begin by understanding the fundamentals of **containerization** and **Docker**. Then, we'll walk through the process of **containerizing a Python application** and deploying it using Docker. The real-world example will demonstrate how to containerize a **Flask application** for deployment, which is a typical use case for web applications.

1. Introduction to Containerization and Docker

1.1 What is Containerization?

Containerization is the process of packaging an application and its dependencies into a **container**, which is a lightweight, stand-alone, executable package. A container ensures that an application runs consistently across different environments, regardless of the underlying system.

Benefits of Containerization:

- **Isolation**: Containers isolate applications from the host environment, preventing conflicts between dependencies.
- **Consistency**: Since containers encapsulate all dependencies, the application will run the same way in any environment (development, testing, production).
- **Portability**: Containers can run on any system that supports Docker, whether it's your local machine, a server, or in the cloud.
- **Efficiency**: Containers are more lightweight than traditional virtual machines, making them faster to start and more resource-efficient.

1.2 What is Docker?

Docker is an open-source platform that automates the deployment, scaling, and management of applications in containers. Docker simplifies the containerization process by providing tools to package, distribute, and run applications in containers.

Key Concepts in Docker:

- **Docker Image**: A read-only template that contains the instructions for creating a container. It includes the application and its dependencies.

- **Docker Container**: A running instance of a Docker image. It's an isolated environment that runs the application.

- **Dockerfile**: A text file that contains the instructions to build a Docker image. It specifies what software to install, how to configure the environment, and how to run the application.

---

2. Creating Docker Containers for Python Applications

2.1 Setting Up Docker

To start using Docker, you need to install Docker on your system:

- Download Docker and install it for your operating system (Windows, macOS, or Linux).

Once Docker is installed, you can verify it by running:

```bash
docker --version
```

This should display the installed version of Docker.

2.2 Creating a Dockerfile for a Python Application

Let's create a simple **Flask application** and Dockerize it. First, let's set up the Flask app.

Example Flask Application (app.py):

```python

from flask import Flask

app = Flask(__name__)

@app.route('/')
def hello_world():
    return 'Hello, Docker World!'

if __name__ == '__main__':
    app.run(host='0.0.0.0', port=5000)
```

Explanation:

- We define a simple Flask app with a single route that returns a message when accessed.

285

- The `app.run(host='0.0.0.0',   port=5000)` ensures that the Flask app listens on all available network interfaces, which is required when running inside a Docker container.

2.3 Creating a Dockerfile

Next, we'll create a `Dockerfile` to define how to build a Docker image for this Flask app.

Dockerfile:

```dockerfile
dockerfile

# Step 1: Use an official Python runtime as the
base image
FROM python:3.8-slim

# Step 2: Set the working directory in the
container
WORKDIR /app

# Step 3:  the current directory contents into
the container at /app
 . /app
```

```
# Step 4: Install any dependencies (Flask in this
case)
RUN     pip     install     --no-cache-dir     -r
requirements.txt


# Step 5: Expose the application port
EXPOSE 5000


# Step 6: Define the command to run the app
CMD ["python", "app.py"]
```

Explanation:

- **FROM python:3.8-slim**: We start with an official Python image (version 3.8) based on a slimmed-down Debian-based image to minimize the container size.
- **WORKDIR /app**: This sets the working directory inside the container to `/app`. All subsequent commands are run from this directory.
- **. /app**: This copies the contents of the current directory (including the `app.py` file) into the container's `/app` directory.
- **RUN pip install --no-cache-dir -r requirements.txt**: Installs the required dependencies, such as Flask, from a `requirements.txt` file.
- **EXPOSE 5000**: Exposes port 5000, the default port for Flask applications, so that the container can be accessed on this port.

- **CMD ["python", "app.py"]**: This defines the command to run when the container starts, which is to run the Flask app.

2.4 Creating a `requirements.txt` File

To specify the dependencies for our Flask app, we create a requirements.txt file:

requirements.txt:

```ini
Flask==2.0.1
```

2.5 Building the Docker Image

To build the Docker image from the `Dockerfile`, run the following command in the same directory where the `Dockerfile` is located:

```bash
docker build -t flask-docker-app .
```

Explanation:

- The `-t flask-docker-app` flag tags the image with the name `flask-docker-app`.

- The `.` specifies the current directory as the build context.

2.6 Running the Docker Container

Once the image is built, you can run the container with the following command:

```bash
```

```
docker run -p 5000:5000 flask-docker-app
```

Explanation:

- `-p 5000:5000` maps port 5000 on the host machine to port 5000 inside the container (where Flask is running).

- `flask-docker-app` is the name of the Docker image you built.

Now, open a web browser and go to `http://localhost:5000` to see your Flask app running inside a Docker container.

3. Real-World Example: Containerizing a Flask Application for Deployment

---

In this section, we will take our **Flask application** and **deploy it** using Docker, which is a real-world scenario where you would use Docker to ensure your application runs consistently across different environments.

3.1 Benefits of Using Docker for Deployment

Docker helps to eliminate the "it works on my machine" problem by providing a consistent environment for running applications. By containerizing a Flask app, you can:

- **Ensure consistency**: Docker containers encapsulate the environment, so the app will run the same way on any machine.
- **Easily scale**: Docker allows you to easily scale applications by running multiple containers, either on a single machine or across multiple machines in the cloud.
- **Simplify deployment**: Docker images are portable and can be deployed easily on any system that supports Docker (e.g., local servers, cloud platforms like AWS, Azure, or Google Cloud).

3.2 Running Docker Containers in Production

Once the Docker image is created, you can run your Flask app in production. For production environments, it's common to use Docker alongside other tools like **Docker Compose** (to manage multi-container applications) or container orchestration platforms like **Kubernetes**.

Here's how you can run the Docker container in production:

1. **Push the Docker image to a container registry** (like Docker Hub, AWS ECR, or Google Container Registry).

2. **Deploy the container to your production environment**, ensuring that the required ports and environment variables are correctly configured.

4. Conclusion

In this chapter, we:

- Learned the basics of **Docker** and **containerization**, which allows applications to be packaged along with their dependencies for consistent execution across different environments.

- Created a **Dockerfile** for a **Flask application**, built a Docker image, and ran the application inside a Docker container.

- Discussed how containerization is essential for **scaling applications** and ensuring portability, especially for deployment in production environments.

Using Docker to containerize applications is a powerful way to ensure consistency, scalability, and ease of deployment. In the next chapter, we will look into **building and deploying scalable web applications** with Docker and other tools like Docker Compose and Kubernetes.

CHAPTER 26

TESTING AND DEBUGGING PYTHON APPLICATIONS

In this chapter, we will cover the essential techniques for **testing** and **debugging** Python applications. Testing is crucial to ensure that your application works as expected and can handle edge cases, while debugging helps you identify and fix issues during development. We will introduce you to **unit testing** with **unittest** and **pytest**, two popular testing frameworks in Python. Additionally, we will explore **debugging techniques** using **pdb** (Python Debugger) and **IDE tools**. To bring these concepts to life, we will work through a **real-world example** of writing tests for a **REST API built with Flask**.

1. Unit Testing with `unittest` and `pytest`

1.1 What is Unit Testing?

Unit testing is a software testing technique where individual units (or components) of an application are tested in isolation. The goal is to ensure that each unit behaves as expected. In Python, two of the most popular unit testing libraries are **unittest** (built-in) and **pytest** (third-party).

1.2 Unit Testing with `unittest`

The **unittest** module is Python's built-in testing framework, inspired by Java's JUnit. It provides tools to create and run tests, and organize them into test suites.

Example: Writing Tests with `unittest`

Let's say we have a simple function that adds two numbers together:

python

```
def add(a, b):
    return a + b
```

To test this function using `unittest`, we would create a test class that inherits from `unittest.TestCase`:

python

```
import unittest
from your_module import add
```

```python
class TestMathOperations(unittest.TestCase):

    def test_add(self):
        self.assertEqual(add(2, 3), 5)
        self.assertEqual(add(-1, 1), 0)
        self.assertEqual(add(-1, -1), -2)

if __name__ == '__main__':
    unittest.main()
```

Explanation:

- **unittest.TestCase**: This class provides a base for all test cases. It includes methods like **assertEqual()** to verify if the function's output matches the expected result.
- **unittest.main()**: This runs the test suite when the script is executed.

To run the tests, simply execute the script:

```bash
bash
```

```
python test_your_module.py
```

1.3 Unit Testing with pytest

pytest is a third-party testing framework that simplifies testing with a more Pythonic syntax and additional features such as better assertion introspection, fixtures, and plugins. It is widely used in the Python community because of its simplicity and powerful features.

Installing `pytest`:

```bash
bash
```

```bash
pip install pytest
```

Example: Writing Tests with `pytest`

Here's the same test case using `pytest`:

```python
python
```

```python
# test_math_operations.py
from your_module import add

def test_add():
    assert add(2, 3) == 5
    assert add(-1, 1) == 0
    assert add(-1, -1) == -2
```

Explanation:

- With `pytest`, we don't need to create a test class or use `assertEqual()`. Instead, we use the simple **assert** statement.

- **`pytest`** automatically discovers test functions prefixed with `test_` and executes them.

To run the tests with `pytest`, execute:

```bash

pytest test_math_operations.py
```

2. Debugging Techniques Using pdb and IDE Tools

2.1 What is Debugging?

Debugging is the process of identifying, isolating, and fixing issues in your code. Python provides several tools for debugging, including the built-in **pdb** module and various features in IDEs like **PyCharm** and **VS Code**.

2.2 Debugging with pdb (Python Debugger)

pdb is Python's built-in debugger. It allows you to step through your code line by line, inspect variables, and evaluate expressions to understand what's going wrong.

Basic Commands in pdb:

- **n**: Next – Execute the current line and stop at the next line in the current function.
- **s**: Step – Step into a function being called at the current line.
- **c**: Continue – Resume execution until the next breakpoint.
- **q**: Quit – Exit the debugger.
- **p**: Print – Print the value of an expression (e.g., p variable_name).

To use pdb, insert the following line at the point where you want to start debugging:

python

```python
import pdb; pdb.set_trace()
```

Example: Debugging with pdb

python

```python
def divide(a, b):
    import pdb; pdb.set_trace()    # Start debugging here
    return a / b

print(divide(4, 2))    # This will start the debugger
```

When you run the script, execution will pause at the `pdb.set_trace()` line. You can then use the `p` command to inspect the values of `a` and `b`, and step through the code to see what happens.

2.3 Debugging with IDE Tools

Many Integrated Development Environments (IDEs) provide **graphical debuggers** that make the process of debugging easier. In PyCharm, VS Code, and other popular IDEs, you can set **breakpoints**, step through code, inspect variables, and even modify code during runtime.

- **PyCharm**: Set a breakpoint by clicking in the gutter next to the line number. When you run the program in debug mode, execution will pause at the breakpoint, allowing you to inspect variables and step through the code.
- **VS Code**: Similar to PyCharm, you can click next to the line numbers to set breakpoints and use the Debug pane to step through the code.

3. Real-World Example: Writing Tests for a REST API Built with Flask

Now that we understand unit testing and debugging, let's apply these concepts in a **real-world example**. We'll build a **REST API** using Flask and then write tests for it using **pytest**.

3.1 Building a Simple Flask REST API

Let's create a basic Flask API that allows users to add items to a to-do list.

python

```python
from flask import Flask, jsonify, request

app = Flask(__name__)

# In-memory store for the to-do items
todos = []

@app.route('/todos', methods=['GET'])
def get_todos():
    return jsonify(todos)

@app.route('/todos', methods=['POST'])
def add_todo():
    data = request.get_json()
    todos.append(data)
    return jsonify(data), 201

if __name__ == '__main__':
```

```
app.run(debug=True)
```

Explanation:

- **GET /todos**: Returns all the to-do items in JSON format.
- **POST /todos**: Adds a new to-do item to the list. The item is provided as a JSON body.

3.2 Writing Tests for the Flask API with `pytest`

To test this API, we can use `pytest` along with **Flask's test client**. The test client allows us to simulate requests to the Flask application without running a server.

Example Test Suite for the Flask API:

python

```python
import pytest
from app import app

@pytest.fixture
def client():
    with app.test_client() as client:
        yield client

def test_get_todos(client):
```

```
response = client.get('/todos')
assert response.status_code == 200
assert response.json == []

def test_add_todo(client):
    todo = {'task': 'Learn Python'}
    response = client.post('/todos', json=todo)
    assert response.status_code == 201
    assert response.json == todo

    # Verify the item is added
    response = client.get('/todos')
    assert len(response.json) == 1
    assert response.json[0] == todo
```

Explanation:

- **client()**: A **pytest fixture** that sets up the Flask test client, which is used to send requests to the Flask app.
- **test_get_todos()**: Tests the **GET /todos** endpoint to ensure it returns an empty list initially.
- **test_add_todo()**: Tests the **POST /todos** endpoint to ensure a new to-do item is added successfully and that it appears in the list when we retrieve it.

3.3 Running the Tests

To run the tests with `pytest`, execute the following command in the terminal:

```bash
pytest test_app.py
```

Explanation:

- `pytest` will discover all functions prefixed with `test_` and execute them.
- It will report any failed assertions and provide detailed feedback.

---

4. Conclusion

In this chapter, we:

- Explored **unit testing** using `unittest` and `pytest` to ensure our Python applications work as expected.
- Learned how to **debug** Python code using `pdb` and **IDE debugging tools**.
- Worked through a **real-world example** of writing tests for a **Flask REST API** using `pytest`, which included testing both the GET and POST requests.

- Understood the importance of testing and debugging in the development process to ensure code quality and reliability.

In the next chapter, we will explore **scaling Python applications** and discuss strategies for optimizing performance and deploying applications in production environments.

CHAPTER 27

FINAL PROJECT: BUILD A FULL-STACK APPLICATION

In this final chapter, we will design and build a complete **full-stack web application**. This will bring together everything we've learned about web development, including **backend** development with **Flask**, **frontend** development with **HTML/CSS**, **database integration**, **API integration**, and **deployment**. By the end of this chapter, you will have built a fully functional web application and deployed it to a platform like **Heroku** or **AWS**.

We will go step-by-step, designing the architecture, setting up the backend and frontend, integrating a database, and deploying the application to the cloud.

1. Putting It All Together: Designing and Building a Complete Full-Stack Web Application

A full-stack web application consists of the **frontend**, **backend**, and a **database**. The frontend handles the user interface, the backend processes requests, and the database stores the data.

Steps to Build the Application:

1. **Backend (Flask)**: We will build a Flask backend to handle the server-side logic and provide endpoints for the frontend to interact with.

2. **Frontend (HTML/CSS)**: The frontend will consist of static files (HTML and CSS) to provide a user interface for the application.

3. **Database**: We will integrate a database (e.g., **SQLite** or **PostgreSQL**) to store data for the application.

4. **API Integration**: We will integrate external APIs if needed, or we will use the backend to handle API requests.

5. **Deployment**: Once everything is set up, we will deploy the application to a cloud platform like **Heroku** or **AWS**.

---

2. Key Steps: Backend (Flask), Frontend (HTML/CSS), Database, API Integration, and Deployment

---

2.1 Backend: Flask API

First, let's create the **backend** using **Flask**. We will build a simple **Task Manager** application, where users can add, update, delete, and view tasks.

Setting up the Backend:

1. **Install Dependencies**:

```bash
bash
```

```bash
pip install flask flask_sqlalchemy
```

2. **Creating the Flask App (app.py)**:

```python
python

from flask import Flask, request, jsonify
from flask_sqlalchemy import SQLAlchemy

app = Flask(__name__)

# Setup the database
app.config['SQLALCHEMY_DATABASE_URI']           =
'sqlite:///tasks.db'
app.config['SQLALCHEMY_TRACK_MODIFICATIONS']    =
False
db = SQLAlchemy(app)

# Task Model
class Task(db.Model):
    id = db.Column(db.Integer, primary_key=True)
    title       =         db.Column(db.String(100),
nullable=False)
```

```python
    description     =     db.Column(db.String(200),
nullable=False)
    completed       =            db.Column(db.Boolean,
default=False)

    def __repr__(self):
        return f"<Task {self.title}>"

# Create the database
with app.app_context():
    db.create_all()

# Routes
@app.route('/tasks', methods=['GET'])
def get_tasks():
    tasks = Task.query.all()
    return   jsonify([{'id':   task.id,   'title':
task.title,   'description':   task.description,
'completed': task.completed} for task in tasks])

@app.route('/tasks', methods=['POST'])
def add_task():
    data = request.get_json()
    task      =          Task(title=data['title'],
description=data['description'])
    db.session.add(task)
    db.session.commit()
```

```python
    return jsonify({'id': task.id, 'title':
task.title, 'description': task.description}),
201


@app.route('/tasks/<int:id>', methods=['PUT'])
def update_task(id):
    data = request.get_json()
    task = Task.query.get(id)
    if not task:
        return jsonify({'error': 'Task not
found'}), 404
    task.completed = data.get('completed',
task.completed)
    db.session.commit()
    return jsonify({'id': task.id, 'completed':
task.completed})


@app.route('/tasks/<int:id>',
methods=['DELETE'])
def delete_task(id):
    task = Task.query.get(id)
    if not task:
        return jsonify({'error': 'Task not
found'}), 404
    db.session.delete(task)
    db.session.commit()
    return jsonify({'message': 'Task deleted
successfully'}), 200
```

```
if __name__ == '__main__':
    app.run(debug=True)
```

Explanation:

- We define a **Task model** using **SQLAlchemy**, which will be used to store tasks in a SQLite database.
- The Flask app has routes for the following:
  - **GET /tasks**: Retrieve all tasks.
  - **POST /tasks**: Add a new task.
  - **PUT /tasks/{id}**: Update a task's completion status.
  - **DELETE /tasks/{id}**: Delete a task.

2.2 Frontend: HTML/CSS

The frontend will consist of **HTML** for structure and **CSS** for styling. We will create a simple UI that allows users to view, add, and manage tasks.

Creating the Frontend:

1. **HTML Structure (templates/index.html)**:

html

```
<!DOCTYPE html>
```

```
<html lang="en">
<head>
    <meta charset="UTF-8">
    <meta name="viewport" content="width=device-
width, initial-scale=1.0">
    <title>Task Manager</title>
    <link        rel="stylesheet"        href="{{
url_for('static', filename='style.css') }}">
</head>
<body>
    <div class="container">
        <h1>Task Manager</h1>
        <form id="task-form">
            <input type="text" id="task-title"
placeholder="Task title" required>
            <textarea    id="task-description"
placeholder="Task              description"
required></textarea>
            <button        type="submit">Add
Task</button>
        </form>

        <ul id="task-list"></ul>
    </div>
    <script      src="{{      url_for('static',
filename='script.js') }}"></script>
</body>
</html>
```

2. **CSS Styling (static/style.css):**

311

```css
css

body {
    font-family: Arial, sans-serif;
    margin: 0;
    padding: 0;
    background-color: #f4f4f4;
}

.container {
    max-width: 600px;
    margin: 50px auto;
    padding: 20px;
    background-color: white;
    border-radius: 8px;
    box-shadow: 0 0 10px rgba(0, 0, 0, 0.1);
}

h1 {
    text-align: center;
}

input, textarea {
    width: 100%;
    padding: 10px;
    margin-bottom: 10px;
    border: 1px solid #ccc;
    border-radius: 4px;
}
```

```css
button {
    width: 100%;
    padding: 10px;
    background-color: #28a745;
    color: white;
    border: none;
    border-radius: 4px;
}

button:hover {
    background-color: #218838;
}

ul {
    list-style: none;
    padding: 0;
}

li {
    display: flex;
    justify-content: space-between;
    background-color: #f9f9f9;
    margin: 5px 0;
    padding: 10px;
    border-radius: 4px;
}
```

3. **JavaScript (static/script.js)**:

313

```javascript
javascript

document.getElementById('task-
form').addEventListener('submit', function(e) {
    e.preventDefault();
    const title = document.getElementById('task-
title').value;
    const              description              =
document.getElementById('task-
description').value;

    fetch('/tasks', {
        method: 'POST',
        headers: {
            'Content-Type': 'application/json',
        },
        body:        JSON.stringify({        title,
description })
    })
    .then(response => response.json())
    .then(task => {
        const li = document.createElement('li');
        li.textContent = task.title + ': ' +
task.description;
        document.getElementById('task-
list').appendChild(li);
    })
    .catch(error   =>   console.error('Error:',
error));
```

```
});
```

2.3 Database Integration

We have already set up the **SQLite database** using SQLAlchemy in the Flask app (`app.py`). When the Flask app runs, it creates a file called **tasks.db**, which stores all the tasks.

2.4 API Integration

The frontend (HTML/CSS/JavaScript) will interact with the backend (Flask) through the Flask API we defined earlier. The frontend sends **POST** requests to add tasks, **GET** requests to retrieve tasks, and **DELETE/PUT** requests to manage tasks.

2.5 Deploying the Application

Once the full-stack application is complete, we can deploy it to the cloud. We'll use **Heroku**, a platform that simplifies the deployment process for web applications.

3. Deploying to Heroku

315

3.1 Install Heroku CLI

If you don't already have Heroku CLI installed, download and install it from Heroku's official website.

3.2 Set up `Procfile`

Create a `Procfile` in your project directory. This file tells Heroku how to run your application.

```
makefile
```

```
web: python app.py
```

3.3 Create `requirements.txt`

Create a `requirements.txt` file listing all the dependencies:

```
bash
```

```
pip freeze > requirements.txt
```

3.4 Deploy the Application

1. **Log in to Heroku**:

```
bash
```

```
heroku login
```

2. **Create a new Heroku app**:

```
bash
```

```
heroku create my-task-manager
```

3. **Deploy the app**:

```
bash
```

```
git init
heroku create
git add .
git commit -m "Initial commit"
git push heroku master
```

4. **Open the app**:

```
bash
```

```
heroku open
```

Your Flask app should now be live on Heroku!

---

4. Conclusion

In this chapter, we:

317

- Learned how to **design and build a full-stack web application** using **Flask** for the backend and **HTML/CSS/JavaScript** for the frontend.
- Integrated a **database** using **SQLAlchemy** to store and manage data.
- **Deployed** the application to **Heroku**, making it accessible to the world.

This final project shows how to combine the different technologies we've learned to build a complete, scalable web application. In the next chapter, we will dive deeper into **advanced scaling and optimization techniques**, ensuring that your applications can handle more traffic and data.

www.ingramcontent.com/pod-product-compliance
Lightning Source LLC
LaVergne TN
LVHW051432050326
832903LV00030BD/3039